THRIVING IN INTERNATIONAL SCHOOLS

A GUIDE FOR LOCAL ADMINISTRATIVE NON-TEACHING SUPPORT STAFF

HENRY WONG

Your feedback and comments on this book are most welcome. Please write to Henry Wong on LinkedIn:

https://linkedin.com/in/henry-wong-bb65481/

OR

Email him at henry@pdacademia.com.

Presented in two distinct sections, the book features the first part that addresses the challenges numerous local support staff members face while adapting to international school environments. It explores the reasons behind these challenges and offers insightful suggestions for thriving in such settings. The second part features contributions from experienced academic and business administrators representing various international schools. They share their insights to enrich the main author's perspectives and delve deeper into the concept of thriving within international school contexts.

This book is often used as a resource for generating discussions during professional development workshops tailored to local administrative support staff. Should you be interested in extending PD opportunities for your non-teaching support staff, please contact Michael Iannini at michael@pdacademia.com, or you can explore further details at https://www.pdacademia.com.

FOREWORD

Any organization, be it an international school or business, is only as good as the people in it. A manager's responsibility is to ensure they employ the right people. They then need to understand, nurture, develop and support their teams to draw on the talents and expertise within the group in order to deliver the best service and results possible. The well-known saying "it takes a village to raise a child" is particularly relevant to any school as it is the responsibility of everyone on campus to provide a safe, supportive and academically challenging learning environment for students.

The non-teaching support team is an essential part of the school's village, and it is vital they know and understand their customers so they can serve them well. As a non-teaching support staff member your main customers include teachers, parents and students.

I have been fortunate enough to have worked with Henry Wong during his time as Business Manager at Suzhou Singapore International School in China. His focus on developing interpersonal relationships and enhancing the non-teaching support team's service orientated approach was a credit to him, the legacy of which continues today. He actively promoted the school's mission of "providing an excellent international education" through his training sessions, coaching and mentoring of staff under his supervision.

Mark Treichel

Educator & Administrator

International Schools in China

TABLE OF CONTENTS

Foreword i

SECTION ONE

Thriving In International Schools 2

A Guide For Local Administrative Non-Teaching Support Staff 2

    Executive Summary 2

    Introduction 3

    Characteristics Of International Schools 6

    The Dynamics Of An International School Micro-Culture 7

    Requirements And Training For Academic Staff In International Schools 7

    Essential Training Concepts For Foreign Educators 8

    Local Administrative Non-Teaching Support Staff Are Often Overlooked 10

    Local Support Staff 13

    Addressing The Issue: A Three-Pronged Solution To The International School Micro-Culture Shock 15

    Selecting Suitable Candidates For The Interview 16

    Organizing An Induction Or Orientation Program For Local Recruits 19

    Providing Insights And Guidance For Support Staff 23

    Building Rapport 30

    Cultivating Relationships With Your Foreign Colleagues 31

Continuous Learning And Growth 32
Understanding And Embracing Different Cultures 34
Developing Trust 36
Cultivating Open Authentic Trust Among Colleagues 39
Building Proficiency Integrity Trust 41
Responsibility Of Academic Administrators And Administrative Leaders In Navigating Micro-Culture Shock: 47
Conclusion 48

SECTION TWO

Insightful Essays From Industry Leaders **51**

Essay #1 - The Difference Makers: Non-Teaching Staff's Essential Role In International Schools 52

Essay #2 - Empowering Yourself In The Changing World 58

Essay #3 - Maximizing Your Positive Impact At Work 65

Essay #4 - Seven Norms Of Collaboration 75

Essay #5 - Playing Your Part In Building An Inclusive Community 86

Thriving in International Schools
A Guide for Local Administrative Non-Teaching Support Staff

SECTION ONE

THRIVING IN INTERNATIONAL SCHOOLS
A Guide for Local Administrative Non-Teaching Support Staff

Executive Summary

International schools generally excel at professionally and culturally preparing new foreign teachers during their onboarding process. Unfortunately, the host country support staff often receive less cultural preparation for their roles. While foreign colleagues face the culture shock of living outside their country, local employees may encounter a different type of culture shock. This book explains the reason for and the extent of this shock and suggests a three-pronged approach to minimizing the challenges.

Although this book is designed specifically for local support staff, it is important for academic administrators and business managers to read it to fully understand the issues at hand. Administrators play a vital role in helping the host country support staff overcome this culture shock.

Introduction

Every member of the school community holds inherent value and makes a significant contribution. My perspective on this has evolved over my two-decade career working in various schools. Through my experiences, I have come to appreciate the meaning behind the well-known African adage, "It takes a village to raise a child," which resonates deeply within any educational setting. It underscores the collective responsibility of all individuals within the school environment to create a secure, nurturing, and intellectually stimulating space for students. In this collaborative endeavor, the support team plays a crucial role.

In our increasingly interconnected world, cross-cultural interactions are inevitable. The seamless movement of people, services, and ideas across borders has facilitated the formation of micro-cultures within a country's native culture. When people from vastly different cultural backgrounds converge, whether in a professional or casual context, it becomes paramount to equip them with the education necessary to foster empathy and mutual understanding.

Cultural education acts as a bridge for effective communication among people of differing cultures. Even when a common language is shared, the absence of cultural training elevates the risk of resorting to stereotypes or misunderstanding one another. Stereotypes propagate the notion that everyone within a particular culture embodies identical traits, thereby negating individuality and marginalizing individuals.

For instance, a prevalent stereotype assumes that individuals of Chinese origin tend to remain reserved and avoid sarcastic yet jovial conversations. Adhering to such a stereotype could lead one to avoid initiating conversations with a Chinese colleague, inadvertently excluding them from friendly exchanges that facilitate relationship-building. To counter the allure of stereotypes and encourage meaningful interaction, a comprehensive study of different cultures within varied environments is imperative.

International schools operating in any country act as epicenters of cultural diversity. They encapsulate a miniature world within the broader global spectrum, reminiscent of a microcosm in a thriving universe. To comprehend this point better, let's consider an analogy: envision a diverse group of people inhabiting a cold oasis in the middle of a scorching desert. The international school environment is akin to the cold oasis, while the surrounding area symbolizes the general populace of the local country in the scorching hot desert.

For local staff members, every day marks a transition as they step through the school gates. They traverse not only physical space but also cultural realms, leaving behind their native context to immerse themselves in the unique micro-culture cultivated within the school. It's important to note that this analogy doesn't imply an inherent superiority of the cold oasis over the desert. Speaking from personal experience as a resident of a desert, I can attest that deserts can offer a pleasant living environment. The underlying emphasis, however, lies in the stark contrast between the cultural dynamics within the cold oasis and those within the desert.

This unique international school culture differs from the broader culture of the host country. It is crucial to differentiate between a subculture and a micro-culture: while a subculture remains a subset of the overarching culture, a micro-culture stands apart. For instance, the millennial culture in the US constitutes a subculture derived from the larger cultural context. In contrast, the flourishing Chinese culture within an African tribal village exemplifies a micro-culture.

Given that international schools function as hubs of cultural diversity, it is imperative to study them closely to devise strategies that mitigate challenges stemming from cultural disparities. However, let's delve into the intricacies of the dynamics inherent to these schools.

"

International schools are a microcosm that has its own micro-culture.

"

Characteristics of International Schools

Defining an international school universally can be challenging, but it is essential to establish a shared understanding between the author and readers of this book. Therefore, a foundational set of features common to international schools includes:

- These schools use English as the primary medium of instruction and administration. English serves as both the language for academic instruction and organizational communication.

- International schools typically hold international accreditations and adopt foreign educational curricula like the Advanced Placement (AP), the Cambridge system (IGCSE), or the International Baccalaureate (IB).

- The teaching faculty primarily comprises individuals educated in Western cultures. Foreign teachers and academic administrators predominantly originate from Western nations and possess native proficiency in English. Among the educators, a minority of host country teachers may instruct their native language as a second or third language within the school's curriculum, with an even smaller number teaching their native language as the first language.

- A significant segment of the student population comprises children from globally mobile expatriate families, including diplomats, professionals engaged with international institutions, and members of non-governmental organizations (NGOs).

The Dynamics of an International School Microculture

To comprehend the cultural fabric of an environment, it is imperative to assess various social factors. Language, educational philosophy, and the background of teaching professionals significantly shape the prevailing culture. In the international school context, where English plays a central role, the dominant culture often reflects Western influences. The widespread use of English as the language for instruction and communication imbues the environment with norms, values, and traditions characteristic of Western culture, which can contrast with the host country's culture.

Requirements and Training for Academic Staff in International Schools

International schools employ foreign teachers who are well-equipped to offer an international educational experience. These teachers typically possess a native-level English proficiency and have at least two years of prior teaching experience. During their induction, these educators typically undergo comprehensive orientation programs designed by the school administration.

Foreign teachers generally arrive with a high degree of professional and cultural preparedness for their roles in the host country. If they are entering a country they have not previously resided in, they often undertake cross-cultural training to prepare themselves for their new role. The primary objective of this training is to facilitate their seamless adjustment to the novel environment, given the disparities between the host country and their home nation. These cross-cultural programs are meticulously crafted to deliver both cultural and professional insights to foreign teachers.

Essential Training Concepts for Foreign Educators

It is crucial to instill the value of cultural empathy within these foreign educators before they embark on their teaching journey in a foreign land. School administrators play an essential role in this endeavor by providing training resources that address pivotal concepts, contributing to the development of a culturally sensitive and adaptable educator. These concepts include:

- **Acknowledging one's own cultural heritage:** This concept encourages foreign teachers to reflect on and comprehend their own cultural background. By recognizing their biases, assumptions, and perspectives, educators can better appreciate the lens through which they view the world. This self-awareness is essential for approaching new cultural contexts with an open mind and avoiding the imposition of one's cultural norms onto the host environment.

- **Fostering awareness of cultural diversity and assimilation:** In a globalized world, acknowledging and celebrating cultural diversity is vital. Teachers must grasp the importance of coexisting with individuals from various cultural backgrounds. Understanding how cultures can blend and coalesce without diminishing their unique attributes promotes a harmonious and inclusive school environment. This awareness also enhances an educator's ability to guide students and coworkers in embracing differences.

- **Demonstrating respect for the host country's individuals and norms:** Respect is a cornerstone of successful cross-cultural interactions. Foreign teachers must comprehend and uphold the cultural norms, etiquettes, and values of the host country. Demonstrating respect goes beyond tolerance; it involves actively engaging with local customs, beliefs, and practices. This respect not only fosters positive relationships with local colleagues but also sets a constructive example for their own students.

- **Identifying and overcoming potential factors that could lead to culture shock:** Moving to a new country can trigger culture shock – a feeling of disorientation and discomfort due to the unfamiliar cultural environment. Teachers must recognize the potential challenges they might face and proactively seek strategies to mitigate culture shock. Adapting to new food, language, social norms, work processes, and daily routines can be overwhelming. By acknowledging and addressing these challenges, educators can transition more smoothly and maintain their well-being.

Typically, these resources are curated from a foreigner's perspective. Individuals considering a teaching role in a foreign country are expected to conduct thorough research to better align themselves with the local environment before joining as educators.

Local Administrative Non-Teaching Support Staff are Often Overlooked

I am aware that certain school heads prioritize cross-cultural education for both their foreign and local staff, offering comprehensive two-day workshops followed by periodic sessions throughout the year. Having spent over sixteen years in the international school industry, engaging with colleagues from various schools in China and Singapore, and interviewing more than a hundred local support employees from across Asian international schools, I have observed a recurring pattern. While extensive training programs are established for academic staff, local administrative non-teaching support staff frequently receive less attention. Though local non-teaching staff might be invited or required to join cross-cultural training sessions alongside their academic colleagues, these sessions often favor engagement with foreign coworkers. This constitutes a significant challenge and an area that requires improvements for numerous international schools in Asia and potentially worldwide.

While culture shock is typically associated with foreign teachers, it is crucial to recognize that local recruits, including teachers, teaching assistants, and non-teaching support staff, may face what I term the "international school micro-culture shock." Most foreign teachers possess prior experience in overseas teaching roles, affording them a degree of familiarity with what to expect. However, this scenario can prove challenging for local recruits. Regrettably, local staff are often inadequately prepared for their roles within international schools, lacking international exposure and experience in vastly different cultural contexts. Insufficient preparation makes assimilation a formidable task. These staff members bring their own values and perceptions of job performance, which can significantly differ from the international school's values and job expectations. Consequently, local staff frequently encounter a form of micro-culture shock. This situation is further exacerbated when:

1. Local staff members who are not adept in the English language may struggle to communicate effectively. This limitation hinders meaningful expression and often places them in uncomfortable situations that demand English proficiency for success. This language barrier can lead to misunderstandings, where the inability to articulate thoughts might be misconstrued as a lack of motivation, confidence, or skill.

2. Some local cultures inherently lean towards less overt communication. For instance, traditional Asian norms prioritize reserve in verbal expression, whereas Western cultures often value verbal articulation. Western-oriented education emphasizes verbal articulation, whereas many non-Western languages involve subtlety and implication rather than direct speech. Without adequate cultural training, this distinction can lead to misinterpretation and further alienation within the international school environment.

3. Local staff members might experience insecurity due to the dominance of Western culture in the school environment. This feeling of inadequacy is heightened when most of the academic staff and administrators, students, and parents align with Western ways of life and speak fluently in English. The philosophy of international education can be unfamiliar to local staff, whose education might have been rooted in local curriculum, values, customs, and norms. These differences can forge conflicts within the school environment, limiting

effectiveness and efficiency. A notable scenario illustrating this challenge involves a foreign colleague making a request that a local staff member finds impossible to fulfill. In their local culture, they might opt for silence to avoid outright refusal to their foreign coworker. However, international schools typically teach assertiveness, encouraging students to transparently decline requests and confidently communicate necessary changes before ultimately accepting them. This disparity can lead to misunderstandings and unmet expectations.

4. The majority of local staff members often assume supporting roles that are non-teaching in nature. Foreign teachers and administrators often hold decision-making authority. This power dynamic can intensify the divide between local and foreign staff, potentially fostering feelings of inferiority among local support staff who play a supportive and service-oriented role. Striking a balance between support and service without succumbing to subservience becomes a nuanced challenge.

The convergence of these factors and uncertainties contributes to a sense among host country employees that they are relegated to a lower status and seen as unequal to their foreign counterparts. This can lead to them feeling like outsiders within their own nation. Mary Hayden's insights in her book "Introduction to International Education" provide a poignant perspective on the potential repercussions if local support staff are disregarded or subject to condescension from students and teaching/administrative staff (Hayden: 149). For some, this disenchantment echoes the intensity of reliving historical colonial experiences.

Local Support Staff

Efficient operation within any organization necessitates the expertise of seasoned professionals. In the past, international organizations often opted for foreign hires in pivotal roles like human resources managers, business directors, and financial controllers. However, the sustainability of this approach waned over time. Sourcing foreign talent proved challenging, compelling organizations to offer substantial salaries to attract them. The financial burden of hiring foreign employees prompted international entities to shift towards localizing their human resources. Leveraging host country employees not only yielded cost savings but also ensured a better fit for managerial roles due to their familiarity with local laws, regulations, logistics, and public interactions. International schools find themselves grappling with a similar challenge. By definition, administrative non-teaching support staff encompass a spectrum of roles including HR, finance, IT helpdesk, facilities management, front desk, buses, catering, cleaning, security, procurement, admissions, marketing, communications, secretaries, and lab technicians.

However, local employees do not encounter the conventional "China culture shock"; they face a distinct phenomenon – the international school micro-culture shock. International schools offer an environment starkly divergent from their local counterparts or even multinational corporations within the same region. It's akin to a micro-culture within the overarching native culture, essentially a foreign enclave within familiar terrain.

The "international school micro-culture shock" can evoke emotions of insecurity, undervaluation, inequality, and diminished confidence among certain local employees. The extensive exposure to the English language may overwhelm them, leading to a self-doubt about effective communication or, worse, any form of communication. This impedes meaningful interaction with their foreign colleagues through collaborative discussions. Beyond language, the international educational philosophy itself may seem unfamiliar, as most local employees have been educated under local curricula. Their approaches to tasks, problem-solving, and interpersonal interactions can significantly differ. These disparities can give rise to conflicts that hinder the school's overall effectiveness and efficiency.

Much like conventional culture shock, micro-culture shock affects individuals variably. Some adapt quickly to minor cultural differences, while others grapple with adjustment. Nonetheless, cultivating a strong sense of self-identity and cultural awareness empowers individuals to navigate micro-culture shock more adeptly and acclimate seamlessly to unfamiliar cultural environments.

While local employees are happy to secure a promising job at an international school, they might remain oblivious to the cultural incompatibility they face when they enter a totally unfamiliar professional ecosystem. Though many host country employees may have prior experience in local or foreign-owned organizations, or even other multi-national corporations, the dynamics of an international school represent an entirely unique paradigm.

It is extremely unfortunate that little research has been directed at addressing the issue of micro-culture shock faced by local employees. The significance and impact of this workforce are monumental for the smooth operation of international schools, especially given their likelihood of longer tenure compared to the transient nature of foreign teachers. Only when non-teaching support functions run without interruption can teachers, students, and parents find satisfaction in the service. In the context of this book, we will briefly present a case for providing adequate training to non-teaching support staff to fortify their foothold within international schools.

> Some host country support staff face the international school micro-culture shock.

Addressing the Issue: A Three-Pronged Solution to the International School Micro-Culture Shock

Recognizing that the environment and interpersonal dynamics within certain international schools may not always foster the equitable treatment of host country nationals as equal colleagues, it is imperative to devise a comprehensive strategy to address this challenge. Crafting an effective plan to navigate this complex landscape requires a delicate balance of sensitivity and wisdom. As respect is a cornerstone value in every educational institution, our approach must ensure that the contributions of host country employees are acknowledged and valued.

While the observation, along with most interviews and surveys for this book, were conducted in China, the issue at hand and its solutions apply to international schools worldwide, transcending borders. This solution encompasses three pillars, outlined below:

1. Selecting Suitable Candidates for the Interview
2. Organizing a Comprehensive Induction or Orientation Program for Local Recruits
3. Providing Insights and Guidance for Local Support Staff

In this book, we will briefly discuss the rationale behind each facet of this three-pronged solution and provide an in-depth exploration of the third element.

1. Selecting Suitable Candidates for the Interview

In the haste to fill vacant positions, there is a common tendency to swiftly hire candidates based on their knowledge and experience in their respective professional fields. However, the critical aspect of ensuring that the candidate is well-prepared to thrive in an international school environment is often overlooked. While a candidate might possess a robust background in their specialized area, the unique challenges posed by an international school setting require a distinct set of skills, cultural adaptability, and an understanding of the institution's ethos.

Failing to thoroughly assess a candidate's compatibility with the international school environment can lead to mismatches between the school's expectations and the individual's working style. This oversight may result in difficulties in communication, challenges in navigating diverse cultural dynamics, and ultimately, hinder the candidate's ability to contribute effectively to the school's objectives. Therefore, educational institutions must prioritize not only the technical qualifications of a candidate but also their capacity to seamlessly integrate into the distinctive micro-culture of an international school. Taking the time for a comprehensive evaluation ensures a more harmonious and productive relationship between the school and its staff.

The selection of the right candidate during the interview process is particularly significant within the context of international schools. The evolution of interviews as a critical hiring aspect stems from their ability to provide insights into an individual's personality traits, interpersonal skills, cross-cultural adaptability, and prior experiences. These attributes collectively determine whether a candidate possesses the compatibility and resilience required to excel in a demanding environment. In international schools, the importance of interviews takes on a heightened dimension, as they play a pivotal role in gauging a candidate's possession of a crucial trait: a multicultural mindset.

A candidate's multicultural mindset is a valuable characteristic that signifies their flexibility and receptiveness to diverse ideas, beliefs, and values. Those with this mindset exhibit a nuanced approach to interpersonal communication, refraining from imposing judgments or conduct based solely on personal comfort zones. Instead, they embrace an adaptable perspective that accommodates a spectrum of cultural perspectives and experiences.

Designing the interview process to effectively assess the multicultural mindset of candidates becomes imperative. The structure of the interview should be thoughtfully crafted to elicit responses and behaviors that reflect this vital attribute. By delving into scenarios that require candidates to navigate cross-cultural scenarios or articulate their outlook on embracing diversity, employers can gain insights into their mindset's depth and authenticity.

Crucially, the interview serves as a platform for employers to evaluate whether a potential candidate has the capacity to not only navigate but also thrive within the intricate tapestry of a culturally diverse and challenging international school environment. The interview conversation becomes a lens through which employers ascertain the degree to which candidates can contribute positively to the school's multicultural ethos and effectively collaborate with colleagues of varied backgrounds.

During the interview, specific questions can be posed to assess the candidate's experience and strategies. For instance: "Can you describe a situation from your previous professional experience where you collaborated with colleagues from diverse cultural backgrounds? How did you approach this collaboration, and what was the outcome?" As a follow-up, inquire, "How do you envision contributing to the multicultural ethos of our international school, and what strategies would you employ to ensure effective communication in a culturally diverse environment?"

Even without direct experience in a diverse environment, candidates can still be assessed for a multicultural mindset. Pose hypothetical scenarios involving cross-cultural interactions and inquire about their approach. Explore their values related to effective collaboration in diverse teams. Assess their willingness to proactively educate themselves about different cultures. Candidates expressing an interest in learning about other cultures demonstrate a proactive approach to developing a multicultural mindset.

Beyond interview questions, observing candidates in scenarios or role-plays mimicking cross-cultural interactions common in an international school setting provides valuable insights. Additionally, allowing candidates to spend time on-site or shadow current staff in multicultural environments offers a firsthand experience to gauge how well they integrate into diverse settings.

In conjunction with identifying a multicultural mindset, another crucial consideration is the candidate's proficiency in the English language, especially if the role requires strong English communication skills. Given that English often serves as the primary language of instruction and communication within international schools, assessing English language skills becomes pivotal. This evaluation can be seamlessly integrated into the interview phase through conversational interactions conducted in English. Effective communication in English indicates a candidate's ability to engage confidently in the diverse linguistic landscape of the school.

In essence, selecting suitable candidates during interviews entails a multi-faceted evaluation that goes beyond technical skills and qualifications. It delves into the intangible qualities that contribute to a candidate's adaptability, open-mindedness, and effective cross-cultural communication. By ensuring that selected candidates possess both a multicultural mindset and strong English language proficiency, international schools set the foundation for a harmonious and thriving multicultural community within their premises.

2. Organizing an Induction or Orientation Program for Local Recruits

This element is crucial in equipping local recruits to navigate the intricate landscape of micro-culture shock. Experts on workplace dynamics worldwide emphasize the importance of such programs, which aim to establish a robust multicultural foundation within new recruits and prepare them for the intensity of exposure to Western norms and practices.

This strategic program is vital because not every potential candidate may inherently possess a deep understanding of a multicultural mindset. An orientation program is essential to cultivate and reinforce this mindset, addressing any gaps and ensuring a unified approach to cross-cultural dynamics. By providing a comprehensive orientation, the school ensures that these employees assimilate seamlessly into the overall workplace dynamics, regardless of their entry point.

A fundamental question arises: Who should spearhead this orientation initiative? Best practices advocate for the collaboration of key stakeholders, including the department head, HR manager, and head of school. This collaboration serves multiple purposes, notably promoting inclusivity by involving various perspectives and insights. Importantly, the orientation should not be perceived as a singular event, but rather as an ongoing process. Multiple follow-up sessions should be scheduled after the initial orientation to sustain the learning curve and reinforce the acquired knowledge.

The timing of the program also plays a vital role. By commencing weeks prior to an employee's official start date, the program establishes an anticipatory and gradual learning trajectory. This is crucial, considering that new recruits might not all start at the same level of understanding. Such gradual progression accommodates diverse learning paces and provides ample time for reflection and application of cross-cultural training insights.

As the program takes shape, it should revolve around pertinent themes and topics to maximize its effectiveness:

- Introducing the international school environment: Comparing local school dynamics to international school norms, emphasizing aspects of cultural exchange, educational philosophy, and curriculum disparities.

- Managing expectations: Exploring the differences in work expectations between local organizations and international schools.

- Embracing the international school demographic: Highlighting the unique characteristics of international school populations, consisting of globally mobile professionals and their children.

- Cultural immersion experiences: Incorporating hands-on experiences that expose local recruits to Western cultures can be highly impactful. This might include cultural exchange events, language workshops, or opportunities to interact with expatriate staff.

- Celebrating cultural diversity: Stressing the importance of diversity in dynamic workplaces, addressing cultural distinctions and their impact on interactions. This module should delve into differences between Western and local cultures. Addressing potential cultural misunderstandings and promoting sensitivity towards these differences can help prevent conflicts and foster harmonious interactions.

- Communication skills and strategies: Providing training in effective communication in a multicultural environment is essential. This could include guidance on cross-cultural communication nuances, active listening techniques, and strategies for clear and respectful communication with colleagues from diverse backgrounds.

- Team Building and Collaboration: Creating a cohesive team that embraces diversity requires skills in team building and collaboration. This theme could include activities and workshops that encourage teamwork, problem-solving, and effective collaboration across cultural boundaries.

- Conflict management and resolution: Equipping new recruits with the tools to professionally manage conflicts with foreign colleagues, fostering effective communication and collaborative problem-solving. Understanding the sources of conflict and recognizing cultural influences on conflicts could also be beneficial.

- Mentorship and support system: Establishing mentorship programs or support networks can greatly assist new recruits in transition. This theme could provide guidance on how to seek mentors, build relationships with colleagues, and navigate challenges with the help of experienced staff.

- Personal and professional growth: Encouraging personal and professional development among non-teaching support staff can enhance their confidence and job satisfaction. This theme could cover goal setting, skill enhancement, and career advancement within the international school environment.

Furthermore, it is imperative to address the existing or potential rift between academic and non-teaching support staff. This divide, often characterized by stereotypes that underestimate the significance of support roles, gives rise to grievances about non-teaching staff exhibiting a lack of initiative, being more reactive than proactive, and not fully engaging with requests. On the other hand, this divide is also marked by stereotypes that academic administrators are pushy and disrespectful, lacking patience in their working relationships. The orientation program must directly confront these perceptions, illuminating the essential role that support staff hold in the school's ecosystem.

In essence, the Induction or Orientation Program serves as a foundational steppingstone for local recruits, equipping them to embrace the distinctive challenges and opportunities presented by the international school micro-culture. Through a meticulously structured and engaging initiative, the program fosters cultural awareness, nurtures unity, and empowers employees to thrive in their roles within this diverse and dynamic educational environment.

3. Providing Insights and Guidance for Support Staff

The essence of fostering a harmonious and effective coexistence between host country support staff and their foreign colleagues lies in understanding and nurturing self-identity. Everyone, whether a local employee or a foreign staff member, possesses a unique identity that defines who they are. Recognizing and cultivating this self-identity is crucial for building self-assurance and facilitating meaningful connections with others. It instills a sense of belonging and offers insights into our role within the school's ecosystem. The significance of self-identity is paramount for all, yet its relevance intensifies the more one engages with colleagues, especially those from foreign backgrounds. For instance, a Human Resources professional typically interacts more frequently with their foreign counterparts than, say, a school chef.

One's identity is molded by a variety of components. For decades, if not centuries, philosophers and psychologists have identified numerous facets that contribute to an individual's identity. Many individuals derive self-identity primarily from work, which includes aspects such as recognition and awards, job satisfaction and fulfillment, professional relationships, a sense of purpose, personal achievements, and career progression.

Deriving one's identity from work can foster a sense of belonging, purpose, and pride. Self-awareness and self-acknowledgment are crucial for understanding one's role in a school. Staff members should identify their role's significance to the school's goals and values. Spend several minutes identifying 2-3 reasons in simple sentences or bullet points why your role is critical to the department or organization then put it somewhere you can see it every day. For example, as a school bus coordinator, you could note: "My role as a school bus coordinator is crucial to the overall success of the school, as I ensure the safe and timely pick-up and drop-off of students, contributing to the daily well-being and the smooth operation of the school." Constantly reminding yourself of these reasons can be beneficial. Additionally, staff members can use reflective practices, such as journaling or self-assessment, which help in aligning daily tasks with school goals and values. Seeking feedback from supervisors and peers provides insights into one's impact on team outcomes and areas for improvement, reinforcing the understanding of their role's significance. Setting aligned goals, engaging in continuous learning, celebrating achievements, and connecting work with personal values all contribute to a deeper sense of purpose and motivation, enhancing self-identity within the organizational context.

Taking an active role in acknowledging contributions and understanding job significance fosters a strong self-identity at work. This approach not only leads to personal growth and professional development but also reinforces one's value and impact within the organization. By embracing these strategies, individuals can cultivate a fulfilling and meaningful connection between their work roles and broader aspirations, contributing to a well-rounded sense of self-identity and purpose.

On the flip side, over-identification with work can lead to neglecting other aspects of life, causing burnout and undue stress. It's crucial to strike a healthy balance by diversifying identity sources, setting boundaries, practicing self-awareness, and seeking support outside of work-related spheres. A well-rounded self-identity integrates various life dimensions, promoting fulfillment and resilience beyond work-related achievements. This multifaceted approach empowers individuals with greater confidence in their interactions and provides ample conversational material, contributing to a positive and enriching work environment.

Here, I have chosen to outline twelve components as a starting point. While this list is by no means exhaustive, it empowers individuals with a greater sense of confidence in their interactions and provides ample conversational material. Once individuals have a clear understanding of their own identity, their confidence naturally grows. They are well-aware of their unique contributions and what they bring to the collective discourse.

> Developing your identity helps build self-confidence and helps better connect with other people.

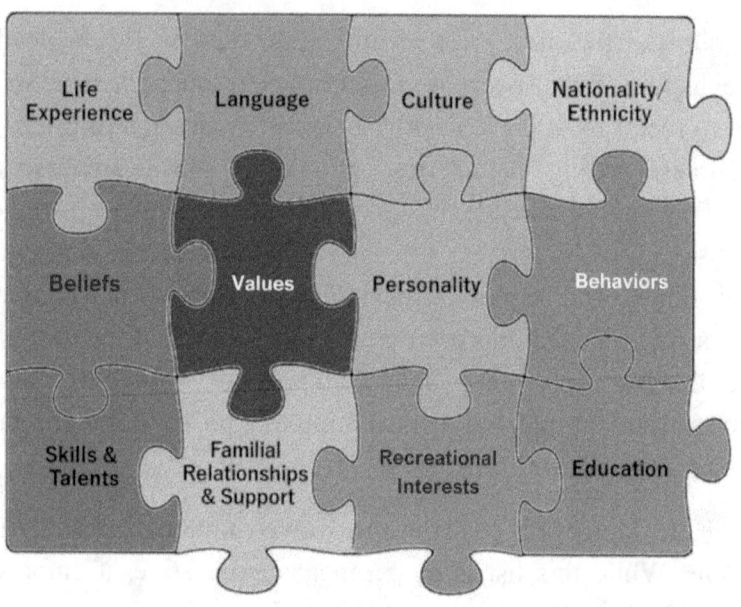

Here are the 12 components that compose your identity:

i. Life Experience – Delve into your personal history. Reflect on your upbringing, cherish your joyful memories, acknowledge any challenging moments, and explore your significant events. Share your first love story or the experience of your initial job. The richness of these experiences provides valuable insights into your essence.

ii. Language – Consider the languages you command, including any dialects. Language shapes your communication style and influences your connections with others.

iii. Culture – Embrace your cultural heritage. Celebrate your regional foods, festivals, landscapes, climate, and more. Your cultural background is a powerful aspect of your identity.

iv. Nationality/Ethnicity – Recognize your nationality and ethnic roots. These shape your subculture and influence how you relate to the broader world.

v. Beliefs – Examine your beliefs, whether they are religious, spiritual, or philosophical. These beliefs mold your values and perspectives.

vi. Values – Identify the core values you hold dear, such as kindness, self-respect, humility, resilience, honesty, and accountability.

vii. Personality – Recognize your personality traits, whether you are introverted or extroverted, a thinker or a feeler. Your personality affects your interactions with others.

viii. Behaviors – Understand your behavioral inclinations. Reflect on your reactions to situations and interactions. Tools like the DISC profile assessment can illuminate behavior patterns and adaptability.

ix. Skills & Talent – Embrace your skills and talents, be they analytical, creative, interpersonal, or technical. Your abilities contribute to your identity and what you bring to the table.

x. Family Relationships & Support – Evaluate your relationships with family members – parents, children, siblings, and spouse. These bonds influence your values and priorities.

xi. Recreational Interests – Engage with your hobbies and passions, whether they involve music, sports, crafts, or other pursuits. Your interests contribute to your multifaceted identity.

xii. Education – Reflect on your educational journey, your favorite subjects, and the teachers who influenced you. Education plays a significant role in shaping your knowledge and perspectives.

After recognizing these components of your identity, consider how you can further develop and nurture them. Reflect on your experiences and their impact on your personal growth. Embrace your cultural background and uniqueness, fostering a sense of belonging and connection with others, including those from diverse cultures. Look for opportunities to share your experiences with your colleagues.

Most people are likely familiar with the prestigious Ritz-Carlton hotel chain. The leaders and managers at this renowned establishment consistently emphasize to their employees that they are serving customers referred to as "ladies and gentlemen." While this term holds a certain grandeur, it carries a deeper significance. The staff members are also recognized as "ladies and gentlemen" who are in turn serving "ladies and gentlemen."

This goes beyond mere semantics. The Ritz-Carlton is resolute in portraying its staff not as mere servants, despite their responsibility for guest service. Instead, they are regarded as "ladies and gentlemen" themselves. In this approach, the Ritz-Carlton fosters professionalism and dignity among its staff.

Similarly, we are far more than a label like "administrative office employee" or "support staff." We should not underestimate or diminish our own value. Embrace confidence. I'm advocating for a sense of pride while maintaining humility. It's important to let go of the notion that Western cultures and people hold superiority. The same applies to one's own culture and people. We are distinct yet equal.

I was born and raised in Singapore, pursued my higher education in the US, and am now partially retired in the US. I spent 16 years living in China, during which I had the opportunity to collaborate with both Westerners and Chinese individuals. I consistently view myself as a bridge between Eastern and Western perspectives, as well as a link connecting the academic and administrative divisions. I wish to share a few insights with readers, particularly if you find yourself as a host country support staff member. While these tips are simple and straightforward, if consistently applied, they can yield significant results. These insights aim to enhance effectiveness in an international school setting, fostering productive interactions with colleagues. While my primary focus is on interactions with foreign colleagues, the underlying principles are universally applicable to all professional relationships.

Fostering an effective working relationship necessitates a level of comfort that can only be achieved through communication. Consequently, the establishment of relationships holds immense importance. Building rapport becomes a fundamental step before embarking on any meaningful connection.

1. Building rapport

Let's start by emphasizing the importance of common courtesy, such as greeting with a simple "Good morning" and a friendly smile. A gentle fist bump can also effectively serve as a colleague-to-colleague greeting.

Engaging in small talk is another valuable strategy. Small talk plays a crucial role in establishing a sense of comfort among colleagues. However, the inclination for small talk is influenced by cultural norms. Reflecting on my seventeen years of professional and personal experiences in China, I observed that the Chinese are generally reserved in making small talk with unfamiliar individuals even though they excel in it with acquaintances. This cultural tendency is shared among many Asian cultures. In contrast, Westerners tend to be more comfortable with this practice. For instance, when I opened a bank account in the U.S. for my new business, the banker engaged in casual conversation with me for about 25-30 minutes, covering topics like the weather, city living, Asian cuisine, travel, and the pandemic. Small talk serves a vital role in alleviating work-related stress and anxiety.

Furthermore, small talk provides a valuable opportunity for individuals to unwind before delving into important discussions or tasks. When a foreign teacher approaches the Finance department for reimbursements, initiating small talk on everyday topics like the weather, traffic, weekend plans, or school events can contribute to a relaxed atmosphere. This practice should be consistently encouraged, particularly within the unique setting of an international school environment.

The creation of the twelve-piece identity puzzle serves an additional purpose. The twelve topics encompassed in the puzzle can function as excellent conversation starters or discussion points.

2. Cultivating relationships with your foreign colleagues

To effectively support and attend to the needs of foreign parents and teachers, it's imperative to familiarize yourself with them and their preferences. Establishing friendships with individuals from different cultures enriches your understanding of their requirements, preferences, and concerns. Knowing someone on a personal level transforms the nature of conversations, making them more courteous and non-confrontational, particularly when addressing issues.

Over the past three years, I've conducted a cross-cultural poll involving more than 300 respondents. The findings unveiled a direct correlation between those maintaining robust working relationships with their foreign colleagues and those considering foreign colleagues as friends. In simple terms, befriending a foreign colleague often leads to positive working relationships with others from different cultural backgrounds. From my perspective, friendship denotes a connection between individuals who genuinely enjoy each other's company and relish spending time together. An illustrative example of friendship is having a companion with whom you engage in shared activities, such as dining out, hiking, watching movies, or simply hanging out.

Naturally, there's no obligation to forge friendships with all foreign teachers. My suggestion is to begin by engaging in small talk with someone familiar, then gradually extend this practice to individuals with whom you feel slightly comfortable. This gradual approach can help you develop the confidence to build connections with a diverse range of colleagues.

3. Continuous learning and growth

Professional development opportunities are often less accessible for support staff compared to their academic counterparts. However, seizing growth opportunities is crucial when they arise. Taking that step, registering, and embracing the learning process are essential. A positive trend is the increasing availability of professional development opportunities for support staff. For instance, in a prestigious school, non-teaching staff were recently included in PD sessions traditionally reserved for their teaching staff for the first time. The school is committed to continuing this practice, running PD sessions for both non-teaching staff and academic staff on their designated PD days in the future.

Beyond conventional workshops, alternative avenues for learning and growth have emerged. A notable initiative is the PeerSphere program, which has cultivated over sixty Peer Sharing and Learning Communities, encompassing various academic and non-teaching administrative roles. These communities provide an invaluable platform for staff to connect and glean insights from peers in similar roles across different schools. This stands out as one of the most enriching professional development opportunities. What sets these communities apart is their ongoing nature, conducting regular online live sessions throughout the year. Instead of relying solely on a single workshop leader, community members learn collaboratively, benefiting from a diverse array of perspectives. This peer-to-peer interaction fosters new viewpoints, develops relationships, and builds trust and camaraderie among participants. Through shared experiences and a wealth of collective expertise, members uncover fresh possibilities and gain profound insights that would be challenging to attain individually. Notably, these communities also offer moral support and promote collaboration, particularly during demanding times.

Another essential aspect is continuously improving one's English language proficiency. While this may seem straightforward, its significance cannot be overstated. I've encountered instances where local administrative staff struggle with English communication. This raises concerns about their ability to effectively engage with their foreign colleagues in work-related matters. Ideally, the proficiency level should reach a point where a person can comfortably discuss issues, present arguments, and express perspectives positively and productively.

In our context, language serves as the gateway to the broader world, with English acting as the conduit into the realm of international schools. The benefits of mastering English are widely recognized. An illustrative case is that of one of my schools, where a foreign teacher conducted a comprehensive 12-week English course for our security personnel and school drivers. This initiative covered essential conversational elements such as greetings, casual conversation, question formation, and giving directions. The program for security personnel and school drivers is an investment in effective communication, cultural understanding, and professional development. It not only benefits the individuals directly involved but also contributes to the overall positive and inclusive atmosphere of the international school.

Adhering to a straightforward life philosophy— "Learn more. Do better"—can bring about revolutionary change for host country employees, significantly expediting their language acquisition efforts and other skills development. Yet, effective communication is the cornerstone of success. Host country employees should feel empowered to seek clarification when facing ambiguous instructions from supervisors or foreign teachers. Gradually, as your command of English solidifies, you will establish a robust presence within the international school setting. This newfound confidence will facilitate meaningful and productive discussions. Likewise, foreign teachers who envision a prolonged stay in the host country should equally invest in learning the local language, strengthening their ties with the community, and enhancing their overall experience.

> Learn more. Do better.

4. Understanding and embracing different cultures

International schools bring together individuals from a rich tapestry of diverse cultures. Familiarizing yourself with these cultures not only fosters appreciation for differences but also facilitates connections with people whose backgrounds diverge from one's own. Increased interaction with individuals from various countries not only enhances communication but also nurtures respect and valuation of these cultural differences.

In his 1957 Nobel Peace Prize lecture, Lester Pearson eloquently stated, "How can there be peace without people understanding each other, and how can this be if they don't know each other?" (Lester B. Pearson College of the Pacific, 1982:9). To cultivate an environment characterized by mutual respect and inclusivity across cultures, both foreign teachers and host country employees should embrace, respect, and acknowledge the nuances of diverse cultures.

Consider this illustration: Upon assuming my role as a business admin director for the first time, and with my HR manager being new to the international school industry, we found ourselves perplexed by teachers frequently inquiring if their salaries had been processed, citing urgent bills to pay. Initially, we struggled to comprehend why these educators lacked savings in their bank accounts to pay their bills. It became evident that Asian cultures emphasize frugality and saving, whereas Western cultures focus on investing surplus funds for wealth growth. Hence, foreign teachers have a limited cash balance in their bank accounts. As our understanding deepened, our judgments transformed into empathy for the teachers' financial circumstances.

From an early age, our socialization teaches us to honor guests. Extending this principle, host country employees must regard their foreign colleagues as guests in their nation. An initial strategy to achieve this is through engaging ice-breaking sessions, featuring entertaining presentations on employees' cultural holidays, cuisine, traditions, and significant aspects. For instance, foreign teachers in a Chinese context should learn about festivals like the Dragon Boat Festival and Mid-Autumn Festival. Similarly, Chinese staff should acquaint themselves with Western holidays such as Anzac Day, Boxing Day, St. Patrick's Day, and Thanksgiving.

Drawing from my experience across three international schools and one bilingual school, a recurring divide between academics (often foreign teachers) and the administrative division (predominantly local employees) is observable. This observation echoes sentiments shared by a former teacher of mine with a decade of international school experience: "I've frequently witnessed misunderstandings between teachers and other staff members, particularly those from the host country, in the three international schools I've worked at. While intentions are positive, there's often a 'lost in translation' scenario on both sides," as aptly articulated by Sarah Hubner.

Beyond professional enrichment, embracing cultural education yields personal rewards. It stimulates intellectual curiosity and nurtures empathy. Cultures offer captivating insights into diverse approaches to life, equipping you to navigate an ever-evolving world with confidence and adaptability.

5. Developing trust

Trust serves as the cornerstone of all relationships, whether they unfold in a romantic or professional context. True collaboration, effective teamwork, and the celebration of diversity find fertile ground on the bedrock of trust. It is an indispensable precursor to any fruitful working relationship, acting as a bulwark against the emergence of a toxic environment riddled with perpetual suspicion, mistrust, and unease. The absence of trust fuels doubt, casting a shadow over the intentions and actions of our colleagues, ultimately undermining the effectiveness and efficiency of a school. Conversely, trust generates a sense of collective eagerness to belong, creating a united front propelled by a shared purpose and a genuine willingness to rely on one another. It instills a readiness to contribute wholeheartedly, channeling our commitment, skills, and energy into the shared objectives.

Building trust is an ongoing endeavor that demands unwavering dedication. The process of establishing trust among colleagues is not a fleeting exercise; rather, it unfolds and evolves over time. While nurturing trust may span months or even years, the erosion of trust can occur in a single incident. Thus, cultivating patience and mindfulness is paramount as we navigate the delicate path of building and maintaining trust.

In professional relationships, trust manifests itself in two distinctive forms: open authentic trust and proficiency integrity trust.

Open authentic trust establishes a profound dimension where colleagues feel secure enough to expose vulnerabilities, admit mistakes, and openly share personal shortcomings. This trust is grounded in psychological safety, fostering a culture free from the fear of judgment for imperfections. It creates closeness and mutual understanding that goes beyond the fear of appearing weak or flawed.

Crucially, open authentic trust is a two-way street. It's essential to demonstrate authenticity by embracing vulnerability, opening up to others, revealing insecurities, and uncertainties, and acknowledging limitations. This act is not a sign of weakness but a demonstration of authenticity and courage, creating a space where genuine connections can thrive among individuals.

Embracing vulnerability is pivotal for trust-building at work. Colleagues who show open authentic trust break down barriers hindering genuine communication. Sharing personal challenges and admitting mistakes engenders empathy and reliability, allowing team members to see each other as real people, and promoting understanding, empathy, and compassion.

Vulnerability catalyzes effective problem-solving and innovation. By acknowledging limitations, individuals create an environment where diverse perspectives and ideas can thrive, fostering a culture of continuous learning. This transparency not only sparks creativity but also establishes a culture of mutual support and shared growth, creating resilient relationships and a workplace culture that thrives on genuine connections.

In the practical manifestation of open authentic trust, colleagues actively admit weaknesses and mistakes, ask for help, and accept questions and input about their areas of responsibility. They give one another the benefit of the doubt before arriving at a negative conclusion, take risks in offering feedback and assistance, and appreciate and tap into one another's skills and experiences. They focus time and energy on important issues, not politics, offer and accept apologies without hesitation, and look forward to meetings and other opportunities to work as a group. Embracing vulnerability becomes a cornerstone of an organizational culture that thrives on genuine connections and resilient relationships among colleagues.

Proficiency integrity trust is built on the foundation of your professional capabilities and ethical conduct. Colleagues rely on this form of trust to believe that you possess the skills, knowledge, and integrity required to excel in your role. This implies not only a confidence in your ability to perform tasks proficiently but also a trust that you will consistently make ethical decisions and uphold the values essential for the smooth functioning of the work environment.

> Two Dimensions of Trust: Open Authentic Trust and Proficiency Integrity Trust.

Together, these two dimensions of trust form a robust framework that underpins effective collaboration and teamwork within a professional setting. Colleagues who experience both open authentic trust and proficiency integrity trust are more likely to engage in open communication, share ideas freely, and work together harmoniously, contributing to a healthy and productive work environment. This dual trust dynamic fosters an atmosphere where individuals not only feel safe to be authentic but also have confidence in each other's competence and ethical judgment, creating a synergistic foundation for successful collaboration and a positive workplace culture.

Cultivating Open Authentic Trust Among Colleagues

First and foremost, let's explore strategies for cultivating open authentic trust among colleagues. It's crucial to recognize that trust is not an instantaneous achievement; rather, it evolves through shared experiences over time, consistent follow-through, and the establishment of credibility. Building trust also requires a profound understanding of the unique attributes of team members. The following activities, drawn from "The Five Dysfunctions of a Team" by Patrick Leoncioni, help facilitate that understanding:

Individual Histories Activity (30 minutes):

This exercise aims to foster moderate vulnerability among colleagues. It is designed to reveal aspects of team members that others may not be aware of, despite having worked together for some time. Questions should be thoughtfully chosen, avoiding overly sensitive topics. Examples could include the number of siblings, hometown, unique challenges of childhood, favorite hobbies, first job, and worst job.

Personality and Behavioral Preference Profile (3 hours)

Utilizing a tool like DISC, this profiling exercise allows individuals to better understand and empathize with one another. DISC provides insights into different personality types and behavioral preferences, enhancing team members' awareness of their own and others' working styles.

Team Effectiveness Activity (60 minutes)

This exercise involves a more rigorous exploration of team dynamics. Colleagues identify the single most important contribution each peer makes to the team and an area that needs improvement or elimination for the team's benefit. Subsequently, each employee shares their evaluation, concentrating on one person at a time. It encourages transparency and provides constructive feedback for individual and team development. It's essential to approach this activity with caution, considering that in some cultures, unveiling a colleague's shortcomings in public is considered taboo. Despite this cultural sensitivity, engaging in such activities is crucial for fostering open authentic trust among colleagues.

360-Degree Feedback

Implemented as a developmental tool rather than tied to compensation, 360-degree feedback allows team members to identify strengths and weaknesses without repercussions. This process provides a holistic view of an individual's performance, incorporating feedback from peers, subordinates, and supervisors.

Experiential Team Exercise

By incorporating trust building activities tailored to the work environment, these exercises go beyond theoretical discussions. Practical, hands-on activities enhance teamwork, communication, and problem-solving skills. These activities should be thoughtfully chosen to align with the specific challenges and goals of the team. Unfortunately, some experiential team exercises, while entertaining, may lack relevance to the actual work context.

Implementing these activities creates a multifaceted approach to building trust. From sharing personal histories to providing constructive feedback and understanding personality dynamics, each exercise contributes to a comprehensive trust-building strategy, fostering a cohesive and effective team (Lencioni, 2002).

Building Proficiency Integrity Trust

Let's delve into the building of proficiency integrity trust. Allow me to share the essential elements, a recipe if you will, consisting of four key ingredients.

1. **Excel in your work.** Competence is paramount within the professional realm. Your employment is grounded in your ability to excel in your role. It's important to gauge your performance not solely from a personal

perspective, as individuals often perceive their work more favorably than others might. Actively seek feedback from both peers and supervisors with an open mind, identifying areas for improvement. Studying how counterparts from other international schools or industries execute similar roles can provide valuable insights. For instance, sending janitors to observe the cleaning staff in a 5-star hotel on a professional development day can yield novel perspectives for them.

The foundation of trust crumbles when professional responsibilities are not met. Exceptional performance not only cultivates trust but also aligns with a willingness to assist, even beyond the boundaries of your job description. Demonstrating an ABCD approach – Above, Beyond, Call, Duty – can significantly elevate trust levels.

Allow me to illustrate this with a compelling anecdote. Dursley, a school bus coordinator, not only excelled in his designated role but consistently exceeded expectations by providing assistance beyond the call of duty, particularly to foreign teachers. Situated in a city without an airport, Dursley's locale required a 90-minute drive to the nearest international terminal, predating the advent of ride-sharing services. Taxis were available but posed reliability challenges, especially when time-sensitive flights were involved. One foreign teacher, concerned about catching her flight, sought Dursley's aid in arranging a private car to the airport due to language barriers. Dursley willingly offered his assistance, leaving a lasting impression. The teacher's gratitude cascaded through word-of-mouth. Soon enough, word spread like wildfire, and other foreign teachers began seeking Dursley's help to arrange rides to and from the airport. This expanded support didn't merely involve arranging transportation; at times, it entailed bridging communication gaps between teachers and drivers and facilitating coordination in instances where language was a barrier. Within six years, he moved from being a bus coordinator to being a facility manager to an operations director.

Ultimately, trust flourishes through not only exceptional competence but also a willingness to go beyond the expected, solidifying a reputation that others can rely upon.

2. **Achieve consistent excellence in your work.** Reliability stands as the cornerstone of both personal and professional consistency and dependability. In the workplace context, reliability involves the unwavering delivery of commitments, meeting deadlines, and executing tasks accurately and predictably. It encompasses qualities like punctuality, follow-through, and a steadfast commitment to producing quality results. A reliable employee or team member is one who can be counted on to fulfill their responsibilities consistently, thereby establishing a sense of predictability and trustworthiness.

The role of reliability in fostering trust at work is pivotal due to its fundamental contribution to stability and effective collaboration. When colleagues can rely on each other to fulfill their roles and complete tasks as expected, it fosters a sense of mutual respect and confidence. Trust is built over time through repeated instances of dependability, as consistent behavior creates a positive track record that others can rely on. Reliability also minimizes disruptions, reduces uncertainty, and enhances overall efficiency within an organization. This is especially crucial in team environments where each member's contributions are interdependent.

Consider this: if you commit to a request with a "yes," do you follow through? Do you subsequently follow up? Worse yet, if a foreign colleague reaches out with a request, and you remain unresponsive – these scenarios underscore the pivotal role of reliability. The continuous fulfillment of commitments, even in seemingly trivial requests, conveys an unequivocal message of trustworthiness. Whether it involves meeting deadlines, promptly responding to emails, or honoring promises made to colleagues, these actions construct a reputation of reliability. By showcasing reliability, individuals and teams not only underscore their dedication to organizational triumph but also establish a firm groundwork upon which robust working relationships and a positive work culture can thrive.

3. **Conduct your work ethically and responsibly.** Integrity is the embodiment of aligning one's actions with values, principles, and ethical standards. It entails steadfastly upholding honesty, transparency, and authenticity in all dealings, both personal and professional. An individual with integrity consistently follows through on promises, maintains a high level of ethical conduct, and remains true to his or her word even in the face of challenges. Integrity is not merely adhering to moral codes; it's a reflection of one's inner compass guiding them to act ethically and responsibly.

In the context of building trust at work, integrity is of paramount significance. It forms the bedrock upon which reliable and credible relationships are established. When an individual consistently demonstrates integrity, his or her words and actions are in perfect harmony. This congruence cultivates a sense of dependability and confidence in their interactions with colleagues and superiors alike. Integrity manifests through actions like meeting commitments as promised, being forthcoming about challenges, and owning up to mistakes.

Moreover, fostering integrity requires a shift in communication dynamics. Rather than casually dismissing a task with a "no problem" when uncertain of completion, embracing integrity involves reframing the conversation. Let your "yes" truly mean "yes," and when faced with tasks you're unsure about, express the need for assistance and clarity. This approach not only maintains transparency but also emphasizes a commitment to genuine collaboration. By openly communicating challenges, seeking assistance, and delivering on promises, individuals with integrity create an environment where trust flourishes. In essence, integrity builds a foundation of reliability, transparency, and mutual respect that is essential for effective teamwork and harmonious workplace relationships.

4. **Cultivate Empathy: Connecting Better through Understanding.** Enhancing your English proficiency and embracing cultural understanding are integral components of effective communication. However, it's equally vital to immerse yourself in the perspective of your foreign colleagues. Consider this: most of them might not be familiar with the local language, and the intricacies of the local culture might elude them. When faced with issues like plumbing in their apartments, they may feel at a loss, unsure of how to navigate the situation or communicate with the plumber. Can you anticipate these challenges and extend a helping hand?

This rings particularly true for foreign colleagues, not because they deserve special treatment, but because they've ventured far from their homeland, leaving behind family and friends to work in an environment that often feels alien. The language barrier, coupled with unfamiliar customs and traditions, can make day-to-day tasks, from talking to a landlord to grocery shopping, immensely challenging. Imagine the frustration and helplessness of not being able to explain an apartment issue to a property manager or decipher an emergency alert message in the local language on their cell phone.

Consider Daniel, our new secondary school principal. During his interview process, Human Resources demonstrated exemplary care, ensuring his comfort from airport pickups to hotel check-ins and ferrying him between meetings and interviews. After securing the position, he drove his own car all the way from Suzhou, where he lived, to the capital, where he would be working. He was going to drive to school from his rented apartment on his first day at school. Although he had been to the school before, he never drove to school. While GPS offered navigation, the matter of parking on campus remained uncertain. Daniel, not thinking to ask, found a preemptive information from HR, who, putting themselves in his shoes, provided parking instructions a day in advance. This proactive anticipation of his needs exemplifies empathy in action.

> Proficiency Integrity Trust: Competence, Reliability, Integrity, and Connectedness.

Responsibility of Academic Administrators and Administrative Leaders in Navigating Micro-Culture Shock:

The responsibility of addressing micro-culture shock experienced by host country employees in international schools doesn't solely rest on the shoulders of the local administrative non-teaching support staff. Administrators and leaders, including the head of school, principals, and bursars, play a pivotal role in recognizing and mitigating these challenges.

To effectively motivate and encourage the support staff, administrators and leaders should establish professional relationships based on respect, acknowledging the individual strengths and weaknesses of each team member. Recognizing that some support staff may struggle with English language proficiency, administrators should approach communication with patience and understanding. Additionally, it's necessary to realize that some support staff may lack confidence in relating to their foreign colleagues; therefore, leaders should offer praise generously and seek ways to encourage them to speak up.

When reaching out to the support staff, administrators must maintain a respectful demeanor, understanding that adjusting to an unfamiliar environment is a shared responsibility. Active listening and comprehending the differences between parties, as well as the reasons behind these differences, are crucial. There should be a nuanced approach to problem-solving, deciding when a locally oriented solution is appropriate and providing support rather than mere redirection. Effective collaboration is a two-way process, and both parties need to actively participate in finding common ground.

Moreover, empowering the local administrative and support staff involves strategies beyond recognition. Complimenting their achievements, even small progress, and catching them doing the right thing can boost morale. Building open authentic trust is also crucial. Leaders should be willing to share their own limitations, admitting mistakes when they occur. This vulnerability fosters an environment where trust can flourish.

An important aspect of empowerment is refraining from solving every problem for the support staff. Leaders often have the inclination to jump into decision-making mode. However, allowing direct reports to analyze scenarios, weigh the pros and cons, and propose solutions not only fosters a sense of autonomy but also encourages critical thinking and ownership of decisions. By taking this approach, leaders create a collaborative environment where the support staff feels empowered to contribute meaningfully to the development of the school.

Conclusion

Fostering an inclusive environment for effective communication and professional growth is a fundamental goal for progressive organizations. This manuscript sheds light on the distinct micro-culture within international schools, underlining the potential micro-cultural shock experienced by host country employees in this unique setting. In response to this challenge, the book proposes a comprehensive three-fold solution, emphasizing the significance of tailored training programs designed to address the specific working environment and challenges faced by host country employees. The book imparts principles that local administrative non-teaching support staff can integrate into their daily work, facilitating assimilation into the international school micro-culture for thriving success. This strategic approach aims to cultivate workplace compatibility and harmonious collaboration among diverse stakeholders. **Whether you are an educator or non-teaching staff, a foreigner or local team member, always remember this: we are invaluable contributors to the school community with much to offer.**

This concludes the first section of the book. I hope it has been helpful to you. Now, please proceed to the second section, which features contributions from experienced academic and business administrators representing various international schools. These experts share their insights to enrich the main author's perspectives, offering a diverse range of experiences and practical advice. Their essays delve deeper into the concept of thriving within international school contexts, providing valuable strategies and firsthand accounts that complement and expand upon the challenges and solutions discussed in the first part.

INSIGHTFUL ESSAYS FROM INDUSTRY LEADERS
ESSAYS

SECTION TWO

INSIGHTFUL ESSAYS FROM INDUSTRY LEADERS

ESSAY #1

Kasson Bratton aptly underscores the valuable contributions that non-teaching staff bring to the international school's ecosystem, highlighting several reasons why they are essential members of the school community. Remember: We are invaluable contributors with much to offer. Kasson also strongly advocates for non-teaching staff's involvement in the JEDI task force to empower them and further bridge the gap between academics and business administration.

The Difference Makers: Non-Teaching Staff's Essential Role in International Schools

By Kasson Bratton

Director of Learning & Deputy Head of School

Nanjing International School

Within our schools, a powerful force operates quietly behind the scenes, shaping the educational environment. This force, composed of non-teaching staff (NTS), forms the backbone of our institutions, ensuring that every aspect of a school's operation supports and enhances the student learning experience. Far from being peripheral figures, these dedicated professionals are central to creating a nurturing, efficient, and inclusive environment where the academic and social needs of students are met with precision and care.

International schools, with our diverse communities and complex logistical demands, present a unique set of challenges that go beyond the curriculum and classroom instruction. It is within this context that the non-teaching staff emerge as pivotal players, orchestrating everything from the subtle nuances of daily operations to the grand logistics of major events and programs. Their roles encompass a wide spectrum of responsibilities, including but not limited to, government relations, security, IT systems, medical care, admissions, and facilities management. Each role, while distinct, contributes to the seamless functioning of the school, ensuring that educational delivery can occur unimpeded by the multitude of potential external and internal disruptions.

Additionally, the diversity of the NTS team, in terms of skill sets, backgrounds, and experiences, adds a rich layer of complexity and potential to the school community. From the meticulous planning and execution of campus security measures to the innovative solutions in IT systems, and from the compassionate care in the medical office to the strategic vision in admissions and marketing, non-teaching staff play a critical role in shaping the student experience. Their collective efforts ensure that the school is not just a place of learning, but a safe, inclusive, and inspiring community where every student has the opportunity to thrive. They are, indeed, difference makers!

The Anchor of Longevity

A striking feature of NTS is their longevity within institutions. Serving as the bedrock of stability, these staff members often hold tenure beyond that of teaching counterparts. In many international schools, the average length of stay for NTS is at least twice that of teachers. This means these members of staff hold not only institutional memory but a profound understanding of the institution's ethos and culture. This depth of experience positions NTS as indispensable navigators, guiding schools through the ebbs and flows of educational trends and societal changes.

Leveraging the longevity of non-teaching staff within international schools is akin to cultivating a garden with deep roots and diverse blooms. Encouraging movement within the organization allows these seasoned professionals to bloom, bringing fresh perspectives and renewed energy to different areas of the school's ecosystem. This mobility not only enriches their personal career journey but also enhances the collective operational dynamic, ensuring a vibrant and responsive environment. Complementing this, the implementation of holistic performance reviews coupled with regularly updated job descriptions ensures that the evolving landscape of educational needs and expectations is mirrored in the roles and responsibilities of the staff. Such an approach ensures that every member of the team is aligned with the school's strategic objectives and empowered to contribute at their highest potential. Furthermore, honoring the service of these dedicated individuals through recognition and celebration acknowledges their invaluable contribution to the school's legacy and future. It also reinforces the message that these efforts are seen, appreciated, and integral to the school's success. Through these strategic actions, the longevity of non-teaching staff becomes a powerful lever, amplifying the school's capacity to nurture a thriving, adaptive, and cohesive educational community.

The Reservoir of Expertise

NTS also represents a deep reservoir of expertise in our schools. With a significant percentage boasting tertiary degrees and specialized qualifications, their skill sets extend into realms that enrich the student, family, and teacher experience. By fostering a culture of continuous learning and professional development, schools can leverage this expertise, promoting innovation and elevating the quality of education offered.

Harnessing the expertise of non-teaching staff in international schools involves creating an environment where innovation flourishes, strategic professional development (PD) is prioritized, and team building is integral to the school culture. By carving out room for innovation, schools empower these skilled professionals to devise and implement creative solutions to complex challenges, fostering a culture of continuous improvement and adaptability. Strategic PD (like PeerSphere) ensures that non-teaching staff not only refine existing skills but also acquire new ones, aligning personal growth with the evolving needs of the school community. This commitment to learning and development underscores the school's investment in its staff as key drivers of its success. Additionally, fostering team-building activities strengthens interpersonal relationships and collaboration across departments, breaking down silos and encouraging a unified approach to achieving the school's mission. Together, these strategies not only leverage the existing expertise of non-teaching staff but also cultivate a dynamic and cohesive workforce capable of navigating the challenges and opportunities of international education with agility and confidence.

Cultivating an Inclusive Ecosystem

At the heart of a thriving international school is its commitment to diversity and inclusion. NTS play a pivotal role in weaving the fabric of this inclusive ecosystem. Through initiatives such as DEI (Diversity, Equity, and Inclusion) and JEDI (Justice, Equity, Diversity, and Inclusion), they contribute to creating a culture where every member of the community feels valued and seen. This commitment to inclusion mirrors the broader aspirations of educational institutions to foster environments where all learners can thrive.

To truly harness the power of inclusion in support of non-teaching staff (NTS) within international schools, a multifaceted approach is essential. Offering targeted Diversity, Equity, and Inclusion (DEI) learning in the mother tongue addresses language barriers, allowing NTS to engage deeply with these critical concepts, fostering a sense of belonging and understanding across the entire staff spectrum. Including NTS in the Justice, Equity, Diversity, and Inclusion (JEDI) Taskforce not only empowers, but also ensures that a diverse set of perspectives shape school policies and practices. The creation of a Staff Representative role dedicated to NTS provides these community members with a formal avenue for advocacy and representation, ensuring needs and ideas are consistently brought to the forefront. Implementing Listening Circles also creates safe spaces for open dialogue, where NTS can share experiences and contribute to the collective wisdom of the school community. Furthermore, an annual survey tailored to NTS captures feedback and insights, providing valuable data to inform ongoing improvements and celebrating the integral role they play in the school's ecosystem. Through these deliberate actions, international schools can cultivate an inclusive culture where every member feels valued and has the opportunity to influence the school's journey toward inclusivity and equity.

Navigating Challenges, Seizing Opportunities

Despite the indispensable role of NTS, many challenges exist. Schools must navigate the complexities of compensation as teacher salaries and benefits have become more competitive in the post-pandemic years, often creating a wider gap with NTS compensation. Additionally, the explosion of generative AI presents an opportunity to work more efficiently, as well as the risk of job loss via automation. A final challenge is addressing the notion of flex time and "work from home," especially when students and teachers are away. How can schools make clear and equitable policies that go beyond the traditional "work to the clock" mentality? Addressing these challenges necessitates a strategic approach, one that recognizes the value of NTS and seeks to empower through professional development and supportive policies.

As international schools continue to navigate the complexities of providing high-quality education in a rapidly changing world, the role of NTS remains paramount. Their diverse talents and unwavering dedication form the cornerstone upon which the success of educational institutions is built. In acknowledging and celebrating the contributions of NTS, schools can forge a path toward a more inclusive, effective, and holistic educational experience.

The narrative of international education is incomplete without recognizing the vital contributions of non-teaching staff. They are the difference makers, the unsung heroes whose dedication, expertise, and commitment to inclusion play a pivotal role in shaping the future of learning. As we look to the horizon of educational excellence, it is clear that the journey forward is one that we must undertake together, valuing and leveraging the diverse talents of every member of our school communities. In doing so, we not only honor the contributions of NTS but also pave the way for a more inclusive, dynamic, and thriving educational landscape.

ESSAY #2

Luo Min beautifully describes the benefits of discovering and nurturing one's identity using the Appreciative Inquiry tool. She also discusses the importance of aligning one's role and interests with the overall goals and purpose of the school, helping non-teaching staff like herself see the significance of their value to the institution.

Empowering Yourself in the Changing World

By Luo Min

Administrative Director

Qingdao Amerasia International School (QAIS)

In recent years, international schools have grappled with significant recruitment difficulties, especially in hiring of foreign employees. The recruitment market has become highly competitive, igniting intense pay package battles among schools. Consequently, the individuals hired often fail to meet the specific needs of the schools, leading to various teaching challenges and staff turnover. Additionally, government policies and stricter regulations have had a profound impact on the enrolment process, limiting the ability to attract students. The COVID-19 pandemic has further exacerbated the situation, burdening the administrative department with additional tasks related to epidemic prevention. This surge in responsibilities has resulted in constant overtime work and a feeling of being undervalued.

Amidst the changes sweeping through international schools, it is natural to question whether this career path still offers the same appeal. However, from an objective standpoint, the evolving landscape of international education in China presents both challenges and positive transformations.

Technological advancements have ushered in new possibilities, enabling remote work, online forums, and previously unimaginable opportunities. Taking extended leave for training sessions, which was once difficult, has become more accessible.

Working in an international school has provided not only personal growth but also a wealth of personal rewards. The education industry's potential to create a profound societal impact is undeniable. International schools uphold well-considered educational philosophies validated in developed countries, often ahead of their time.

After eight years of dedicated service in my international school, I find myself brimming with energy, optimism, and anticipation. These heartfelt emotions are a testament to the school's vibrant cultural atmosphere that has nurtured my professional growth. In this article, I am excited to share a valuable tool that has become an integral part of our school's employee training, student inquiry, and parent workshops: "Appreciative Inquiry (AI)."

Appreciative Inquiry (AI) is a powerful and transformative concept, first developed in the 1980s by David Cooperrider and Suresh Srivastva. It empowers individuals and organizations to envision a future filled with positivity, growth, and meaningful change. AI's foundation rests on three key tenets: appreciation, inquiry, and wholeness. These principles form the bedrock of the AI model, driving the process of self-discovery and collective improvement for individuals and teams alike.

Appreciation: At the heart of AI is the act of recognizing the best in people and organizations. It draws upon their strengths and accomplishments, providing a solid foundation upon which to build a brighter future.

Inquiry: Central to AI is the art of asking questions. Embracing an attitude of curiosity and a thirst for discovery. AI revolves around four fundamental questions: "Who am I?", "What do I like?", "What am I good at?", and "What life and work experiences have supported and amplified my strengths?" By exploring these questions, individuals embark on a journey of self-discovery and personal growth.

Wholeness: The principle of wholeness in AI emphasizes the importance of engaging participants from all levels of an organization. By involving everyone, AI creates an inclusive and collaborative environment where diverse perspectives contribute to positive transformation.

Within the context of Amerasia International School, AI has proved to be a pivotal tool in empowering high school students, staff, and even parents on their respective journeys of exploration and development. Through each stage of the Middle Years Programme (MYP) to the Diploma Programme (DP), students engage with these questions, fostering continuous growth and self-awareness.

The school's commitment to the AI model has profoundly influenced the personal growth and development of its staff, and I can attest to this through my own journey. My career began in Shanghai, where I attended high school at Shanghai Jiao Tong University Affiliated Middle School. Pursuing my interest in language and literature, I completed my undergraduate studies in German at Beijing Foreign Studies University and furthered my education with a master's degree in translation studies from the University of Bonn in Germany. My career took me to various roles, including a Sino-German trading company in Bonn and collaborations with government agencies in Shanghai and Beijing. In 2015, I joined Qingdao Amerasia International School, and my time here over nearly a decade has been a transformative experience.

Despite my academic qualifications and work experience, I found myself lacking a profound sense of purpose. My time at Amerasia triggered a shift in perspective, immersing me in the dynamic and innovative environment of an international school, leading me to reflect on my goals and passions. Gradually, exposure to the IB education philosophy introduced me to the ten IB learner profile attributes, which deeply resonate with me now. Concepts such as being open-minded, balanced, reflective, caring, risk-takers, knowledgeable, and principled, alongside the Montessori peace education, exemplified the most crucial mission and direction of education. These values motivated me to explore and discover a sense of purpose.

Transitioning from a relatively straightforward business environment to Amerasia's rich and diverse culture, I quickly realized the multifaceted demands it placed on individuals. The fast-paced nature of the work necessitates constant focus, communication, and collaboration across various departments, demanding good physical stamina to keep up with the pace. Ironically, when I first joined Amerasia, I frequently fell ill, often catching colds and experiencing fevers. However, witnessing the self-discipline and dedication of the teachers and principals inspired me to prioritize physical well-being. Engaging in physical activities I enjoyed, such as yoga and dance training, not only improved my health but also sparked personal interests that contribute to my overall growth.

Amerasia International School fosters an environment where artistic expression thrives, not only for students but also for staff members. Initially disconnected from drawing and painting, I found myself unexpectedly drawn into an art workshop organized by the school's Wellness committee. Guided by an art teacher, I completed a vivid and amusing self-portrait that was later exhibited during the school's art week. This small endeavor proved transformative, particularly during the pandemic period when remote work and social isolation prevailed. As a result, I delved deeper into the world of art by enrolling in an online colored pencil drawing course, finding solace and healing in every finished artwork. This experience taught me the value of trying new things, embracing the courage to explore unfamiliar territories, and realizing the hidden talents within ourselves.

As I continued my journey at Amerasia, I began bringing my hobbies and strengths to the school community. My joy for flower arranging led me to learn various floral design techniques, which I now utilize to adorn the school lobby's front desk and create themed floral displays for school events. Sharing what I love not only adds warmth and beauty to the surroundings but also enhances the overall environmental quality. Engaging in this creative aspect of contribution brings immense joy and a sense of fulfilment, inspiring me to continually explore new ways to make a positive impact within the school community.

The combination of personal growth, self-discovery, and embracing passions has made my journey at Amerasia International School immensely rewarding, affirming the power of Appreciative Inquiry in fostering a sense of purpose and fulfillment in one's career.

Appreciative Inquiry has proven to be a transformative force, requiring active involvement from all stakeholders, and leaving a positive impact on the school community. As a member of Amerasia's administrative team, I have personally experienced the power of AI in fostering teamwork and collaboration to fully utilize our abilities. While teachers and students put up the school's musicals, our administrative team takes on a range of crucial tasks, from project planning and promotion to community engagement and ticket sales. This collective effort results in a work of art completed by the entire school, with the shared sense of accomplishment evident as we hum the familiar show tunes together. This exemplifies the strength of collective efforts in creating something wonderful and meaningful for the community.

Another noteworthy event that showcases the spirit of Appreciative Inquiry at Amerasia is the annual International Day. This celebration exemplifies the core principles of AI, relying on the contributions of staff, teachers, students, and parents. The administrative team plays a vital role in creating a platform for everyone to participate and showcase their talents, promoting unity, diversity, and cultural exchange. This event becomes a manifestation of AI principles, fostering an atmosphere of appreciation and collaboration throughout the entire community.

The school's commitment to fostering an innovative spirit and embracing new challenges aligns with the essence of Appreciative Inquiry. Working alongside Chinese and foreign principals, employees witness the implementation of the school's educational purpose and philosophy in action, benefiting every student, employee, and parent. This continuous pursuit of breaking norms and exploring new areas, like the creation of the inspiring yearbook themes, reflects the forward-thinking nature of AI, promoting unity and resilience within the community.

Through the practice of Appreciative Inquiry, we have discovered our passions and strengths, broadened our perspectives, and continuously explored new fields. This process has gradually improved our personal abilities, but AI's impact doesn't end there. To fully empower ourselves and others, we must collaborate with one another, set altruistic goals and dreams, selflessly serve our community, and create new value for everyone.

I invite you to embark on this journey of discovery, appreciation, and collective empowerment, and be surprised by the greatness we can achieve when we join forces and uplift one another.

ESSAY #3

Claire Peet offers powerful, practical tools and strategies to help non-teaching staff thrive in challenging situations. She also highlights the importance of self-awareness in her advice. Non-teaching staff can make a significant difference in their workplace.

Maximizing Your Positive Impact at Work

Claire Peet

Senior Manager, Learning & PD and Quality Assurance

Yew Chung Education Foundation

    Are you ready to unleash your full potential and make a lasting difference in your workplace? Maximising your positive impact at work may seem like a daunting task, given the challenges that surround us – the dynamics of the environment, the interactions with others, and even our own inner struggles. It's not as simple as plastering on a smile or adopting a "just be positive" mantra. There's so much more at play.

Let's begin with an undeniable truth: You are brilliant. Just by being yourself, you radiate brilliance. The work you do, and the contributions you make to education and your workplace – all reflect the brilliance within you. Your reservoir of gifts and strengths knows no bounds. When it comes to maximising your positive impact, it starts with recognizing the incredible individual that you are, appreciating the tremendous value you bring, and understanding the immeasurable potential you possess.

I invite you to embark on a transformative journey – a journey that will enable you to bring forth your most brilliant self at work. Together, we'll explore practical tools and strategies that will allow you to unleash your superpowers, captivating the world with your unique talents. It's time to embrace who you are, to embrace your greatness. I hope that I can inspire you today and take something away that helps you have a positive impact at work.

It's crucial to invite others into your life while, above all, appreciating yourself. Being appreciated by others is important, but I firmly believe that at the core of it all lies fostering positive self-talk within yourself – genuinely recognizing the value you bring to your own life and the lives of others. We often tend to be excessively hard on ourselves. A common trait many share is the need to please others and seek approval and appreciation. Consequently, when our self-perception is challenged, it can feel deeply personal, triggering self-doubt and self-deprecation. If nothing else, I want you to know that you are exceptional, unique, and deserving of contentment.

So, let's start with a brief, yet impactful story – an analogy that was recently shared with me and left a profound impression. I thought, "Wow, this is a remarkable tale for anyone currently grappling with workplace challenges." It's a story about a baby elephant in a circus, taken by the circus master to be trained in performing tricks every day. After the training sessions, the elephants are brought back to their pen and chained to a post right next to the mother elephant.

The mother elephant has become accustomed to the process and silently complies with the circus trainer. However, the baby elephant despises being chained up, causing distress. It's all new to them, prompting kicking and howling. After a while, they realize that their resistance leads nowhere, and they calm down. They gradually become conditioned to the situation, obediently accepting it. Over time, this routine repeats daily. As the elephant grows and becomes stronger, it becomes physically possible for them to break free from the chain. However, they never do. Day after day, they return to the post in their pen, alongside their mother. The circus trainer puts the chain around their leg., and they simply accept it. They could break the chain if they tried, yet they reach a point where the circus trainer doesn't even need to lock the chain anymore because the elephant has become conditioned to the routine and expectation.

This story offers insight into our behaviour, or how we can behave, in the workplace. Take a moment to reflect: Who might you be in this scenario? Perhaps you're the baby elephant, conditioned by the system, no longer questioning, simply staying in your lane, doing your work, and going home. Maybe you're the mother elephant, reinforcing the expectation, compliant, and emphasising what the baby elephant should do. You've witnessed the baby elephant's response and thought, "Don't worry, you'll get used to it. There's no point in trying to change the situation." Or perhaps you're the circus master or trainer, unwaveringly insisting on doing things a certain way. When someone asks, "Why do we do it like this?" do you find yourself responding with, "That's the way it's always been done?"

You may be an observer, a spectator, or someone entirely different. Consider if there is a role in this analogy that resonates with you. It's not for me to tell you who you are in this scenario, but I encourage you to reflect and think.

Does this story resonate with you? Do you see parallels in your workplace, or even within your social circles or family? If it strikes a chord, I'd like to offer you some tools that can make a difference. These tools will help you infuse positivity into your workplace, recognize opportunities for change, and fully embrace your brilliance. So, let's explore some practical strategies to achieve that.

All these tools require a certain level of self-awareness and self-work, which is often overlooked or neglected. Self-awareness is conscious knowledge of one's own character, feelings, motives, and desires. It involves understanding not only what triggers you, but also *why* it triggers you. It can be challenging to hold a mirror up to yourself, but it is essential. When it comes self-development, we often look externally and blame others, saying things like "They caused this" or "He said" or "She made me feel." However, when something doesn't work for us or triggers us in some way, it takes greater insight and awareness to look inward and ask, "What is this about?" "Why do I find this confronting?" "How can I change this narrative?" "What is within my control?" "What is happening here?" "Why am I reacting this way?" "How does this connect to my sense of self, my values, my beliefs, my experiences?"

Therefore, I want to emphasise that the first step in using these tools is cultivating self-awareness and starting to ask these inner questions.

I'd like to share three instantly usable tools with you.

The first tool for maximising your positive impact at work is to avoid fuelling toxicity. We all know what this looks like in our own work context. It's all too easy to contribute to negativity, to get drawn into negative talk and complaints that are common in the workplace.

My challenge to you is: How can you create a space for positivity? How can you foster a positive impact and remove negative energy? It's not your responsibility to change others or their behaviour or their perception. You cannot control of how others feel or what they project, but you have complete control over how you respond to it. One key way to do this is to focus on possibilities rather than problems.

Recently, there have been distinct camps in conversations about Artificial Intelligence (AI). Some people approach AI with fear, perceiving it as a significant shift that poses a tremendous threat. It's understandable to feel that way, but this fear-based perspective tends to focus on the negatives and problems rather than the possibilities. It also stems from a sense of lack of control. AI can seem threatening when our understanding is limited and media coverage fuels fear, especially when it comes to job security. However, many of the perceived concerns around AI are beyond our influence. Most of us are not in a position to challenge big tech or drive global AI policies. Therefore, we should not let these factors overwhelm us. Instead, let's focus on finding the good in this situation. A helpful approach is to ask yourself, "What is within my control here?" or "What positive impacts can I see?"

I also encourage you to be contagious, but in a positive way. How can you bring your brilliance and positivity into the workplace?

One effective way to do this is by redirecting conversations when someone gets caught in a negative cycle or engages in negative talk. Simply ask, "How do you want to move forward?" This helps shift the focus from the spin and negativity to possibilities and solutions. We all have colleagues who seem to have nothing positive to say and can influence the mood of the entire team. It may feel challenging to be happy around these individuals but remember that it is not your responsibility to change their mindset or solve their problems. However, it's important to recognize that what you focus on grows. Just as negativity spirals, positivity can also spiral. How can we break the cycle of negativity and support ourselves and others? Modelling is key. Show gratitude to yourself and others. Express appreciation for a team member and be specific about what they did.

The second tool that I want to share with you is about reframing, which is closely related to self-awareness piece and inner work. One of the most profound lessons I learned a few years ago is that our thoughts create our emotional responses when we experience something. It's not the specific experience itself that we get hung up on, but rather the immediate emotional reaction triggered by our thoughts.

For instance, recently a senior colleague criticized my communication with an event speaker, stating that it wasn't professional and not how she would have done it. My initial reaction was anger and hurt. I felt that she had criticised my work and undermined me by discussing it with my boss. However, upon reflection, I realized that it was my own reaction and the story I was telling myself, rather than the actual impact of her words. Brené Brown talks extensively about this, explaining that feedback often triggers our perception of what is implied rather than the feedback itself.

In my mind, I immediately jumped to the question "What does this say about me?" The story I told myself was that my boss and other senior individuals would view me as incompetent. I worried that my credibility would be tarnished, and I felt like a weak link. But, it's important to recognise that these were implications and stories I created, not the objective truth of what was said. For me, credibility is crucial, so this feedback hit my self-confidence and belief in myself. It's essential to ask ourselves if something is a fact or an opinion. The feedback shared with my manager was someone's opinion, and I cannot control that. I cannot even control my boss's own opinion. All I can do is assess the situation objectively and not let the stories and implications govern my reaction and self-talk.

To shift your perspective, try to detach yourself from the scenario. I recently came across a question where someone asked, "What do you do when a parent is literally shouting in your face?" The key is to recognise that they are not shouting at you as a person, even if they are making it personal. They don't know you. They are upset about the situation, and they are projecting their emotions onto you. By separating yourself from the scenario and acknowledging that it's just someone venting their emotions, you can avoid taking it personally, even though it may feel that way. Step back and remove your personal identity from the situation.

Take a helicopter view and look at the scenario from a higher perspective.

We must be aware that whenever someone triggers us with anger, frustration, or jealousy, it's about our own issues, not about them. They might have done or said something that triggered us, but we have to take ownership of how we respond to it. There is immense power in realising that it's about us and that no one can make us feel a certain way. We have the choice to decide how we respond and show up. This realisation brings freedom, knowing that nobody has control over us. We all encounter people who trigger us, judge us, hold opinions about us, and reflect our deepest fears. It can be painful when they express judgment or criticism. However, when others approach us with their judgment, anger, or frustration, it's a reflection of how they are feeling, projected onto us. We can't control what others say or do, but we have complete control over our response and whether we internalise it or let it go. You have full control over what you allow to fill your emotional backpack. Don't let others burden you with their emotions. Let it go. I understand that this is not easy. It requires practice and effort. However, doing so will liberate you from the weight of carrying everyone else's emotions, beliefs, and needs.

The final tool I want to share with you is called the "stop technique" described by Lia Garvin in her book 'Unstuck'. The stop technique encourages us to pause in moments of stress or fear. It emphasises the importance of stopping the momentum, taking a step back, and gaining a broader perspective.

Step back

Think

Organise your thoughts

Proceed

Stepping back, physically or metaphorically brings space and allows more to come into view, you buy yourself some time to think and such thinking benefits from a widened perspective that can only come from turning down the heat of the moment. This is crucial because during stressful situations, our ability to think rationally is compromised as blood flow is diverted from our brains. It's a natural response deeply ingrained in our genetics. Unfortunately, when we need to be most mentally sharp, we often find ourselves at our least capable. Our thinking shuts down while our bodies handle the perceived threat, overwhelming our senses. By stepping back and giving ourselves time to think, we can restore brain function, regain control and organise our thoughts. This transition from panic to control is facilitated by the simple act of pausing.

Creating that pause can be as easy as stating that you need time to investigate and will get back to someone. It's about granting yourself the opportunity to step back and organise your thoughts. Alternatively, in the moment, you consciously check in with yourself and count to ten. This technique helps ground you, making you better equipped to proceed with an appropriate action or even inaction. It enhances your awareness of your choices and actions.

Even if you later realise that you could have handled the situation better or made a different choice, it is acceptable. By practising the stop technique, you are nurturing your self-awareness and facilitating personal growth and learning. You are responsive to the lessons that life presents. A good friend and colleague reminds herself of the stop technique by drawing a stop sign in the corner of her notepad. This subtle note-to-self is meaningless to observers but acts as a visual reminder to use the tool when meetings are getting heated and she feels herself losing her calm.

So, those are the three simple techniques; the stop technique, reframing, and how to avoid feeding toxicity in your workplace that I believe can have a huge impact on how you maximise your positive impact at work. While simple in nature, applying the tools is not always easy, but I encourage you to persevere with them and let the magic happen. You cannot change others, but you can change how you respond them. Let your brilliance shine through.

Brown, B, 2018. Dare to Lead: Brave Work. Tough Conversations. Whole Hearts. Vermilion

Garvin, L. 2022. Unstuck: Reframe Your Thinking to Free Yourself from the Patterns and People that Hold You Back. Media Lab Books.

ESSAY #4

In international schools, collaboration and effective communication are essential. Christina Song, with a quarter-century of experience in education, shares valuable insights into navigating communication challenges with colleagues and parents. Drawing from her extensive background, she presents seven key principles to enhance communication. Christina also identifies practical scenarios relevant to the school context, providing opportunities to apply these principles in real-life situations.

Seven Norms of Collaboration

By Christina Song

Admissions & Administrative Offices Manager

International School of Tianjin, China

    I have been working at the International School of Tianjin for more than twenty-five years. I started as a teaching assistant in elementary school and later became the Secondary School Secretary. In 2004, I moved into my current position as the

Admissions and Administrative Offices Manager. Additionally, I also serve as the secretary for the school Director and the Recording Secretary for the school board. Since 2011, I have been invited multiple times as a facilitator for the joint accreditation visit of the Council of International Schools (CIS) and the Western Association of Schools and Colleges (WASC), participating in and completing accreditation tasks for international schools in China and overseas. Furthermore, I am the school's chief translator and a bridge between the school and various stakeholders, including faculty, students, parents, government officials, and other external parties.

First, let's explore some of the common awkward communication situations that many of us might encounter in various settings:

- Interruptions: Being cut off while speaking, not allowing you to finish your thoughts and ideas.

- Fast-paced speech with unclear logic: Difficulty following someone's rapid and incoherent train of thought.

- One-sided demands without feedback: Feeling unheard as the other person only focuses on their own opinions without considering yours.

- Emotional outbursts: Dealing with intense emotions, such as anger or frustration, that create an uncomfortable atmosphere.

- Forceful and inconsiderate tones in front of many people: Aggressive or insensitive behavior in public settings, making others uncomfortable.

- Intrusive personal questions: Asking overly personal or invasive questions, making others feel uneasy.

- Uneven participation in meetings: Some individuals dominate discussions while others remain silent, creating an unbalanced dynamic.

Now, let's move on to the Seven Norms of Collaboration[1][2], which are also communication norms. They are also known as "7P norms" for short, as each norm's first letter starts with the letter "P". These norms have been refined over more than ten years of research by many professionals and have several versions, with similar content. Our goal in learning these norms here is to facilitate group discussions, conflict resolution, and difficult conversations. We need to practice and use these communication strategies to improve our personal communication skills proactively and consciously. When engaging in difficult conversations or facing conflicts, such as dealing with emotionally charged parents or someone making offensive remarks, we may not be able to change their mindset and behavior, but we can positively influence them by consciously using these strategies and guiding them toward rational expression.

The Seven Norms of Collaboration are as follows:

1. *Pausing:* Taking a moment before responding or asking a question allows time for reflection and enhances dialogue, discussion, and decision-making.

Rushing into conversations, especially when tackling complex or sensitive topics, should be avoided. Instead, invite the other person to a relatively private space and offer them tea or coffee

---

[1] Baker, W., Costa A. L., & Shalit, A. (1997). The norms of collaboration: Attaining communicative competence.
[2] Norms of Collaboration Annotated © Center for Adaptive Schools, www.adaptiveschools.com

to help them emotionally calm down. While they speak, we should listen attentively, using eye contact, body language, and posture to convey full engagement. Once they finish sharing, we can offer our input. This approach not only slows down the pace of the conversation and soothes emotions but also demonstrates our appreciation for their thoughts. Before speaking, take a brief pause of about 3-5 seconds, especially for thought-provoking questions. Inform the other person that you will carefully consider their thoughts and opinions and promise to provide feedback later.

2. **Paraphrasing:** Paraphrasing what we have just heard shows respect for the other person and ensures active listening. This critical communication skill allows our conversation partner to verify if we have correctly understood their points. Paraphrasing involves summarizing and interpreting their words in our own language. Use different words or phrases, such as "Your suggestion is..." or "Is your concern about...?" to demonstrate your effort to comprehend their words. This shows respect and helps diffuse any angry emotions they might be experiencing.

3. **Posing Questions:** The art of posing questions serves two intentions: to explore and specify thinking. Use questions to delve into perceptions, assumptions, and interpretations, encouraging others to examine their thought processes.

Clarity and precision are crucial to elucidate any points that may not have been fully explained and to ensure a shared understanding of key terms, preventing deviations from the topic. Sometimes, the information provided by the other person might be vague. For example, when someone says, "All parents think this way," it's essential to inquire specifically about which parents they are referring to. Differences in culture, education, and cognition can lead to varying understandings and feelings about matters. Understanding which parents or specific backgrounds hold certain opinions can help us further discuss and resolve issues.

When posing questions, be mindful of your tone and demeanor to avoid coming across as challenging or confrontational. We should avoid using questions that target individuals, such as "What do you mean exactly?" or rhetorical questions like "Don't you know the school rules?" The purpose of questions is to explore and clarify ideas, not to escalate conflicts or provoke anger. Instead, we aim to foster an environment of open dialogue and mutual understanding.

4. *Putting Ideas on the Table:* In collaborative conversations, it is vital for all participants to be willing to share their own ideas and opinions. Without everyone's active contribution, meetings or discussions cannot lead to meaningful conclusions or progress on any subject.

Expressing ideas directly requires confidence and courage. Before speaking up, consider the relevance and appropriateness of our content, avoiding going off-topic or being unclear. Moreover, when noticing others remaining silent, encourage them to voice their thoughts. Whether you are the organizer or a participant in a meeting, proactively inquire about others' ideas. Even a simple statement like "I agree" shows engagement and reflection on the discussion, rather than being a passive listener. Ultimately, staying silent or withholding ideas hinders the healthy development of any organization and undermines the establishment of a learning community. In situations where different opinions arise, focus on providing constructive suggestions rather than outright negating others' views. Using phrases like "I disagree, no matter what you say, I won't agree!"

or remaining silent during disagreements and then refusing to accept the meeting outcomes are unhelpful approaches.

Consciously and actively expressing your ideas to create an environment conducive to open and honest dialogue, welcoming fresh perspectives from new colleagues or individuals from other departments. Their ideas are equally valuable, and listening to their thoughts helps us avoid falling into fixed thinking patterns that can result from working in the same department for a long time. If you are a new employee or someone who worries about the appropriateness of your contributions and fears being mocked, remember: the purpose of our dialogue is to share our ideas, leverage collective wisdom, and ultimately achieve results. We are all colleagues, and ideas themselves have no inherent right or wrong. So, do not hesitate to speak up and share your thoughts.

5. ***Providing Data:*** Offering data in various forms, both qualitative and quantitative, is essential in supporting group members to construct a shared understanding from their work.

Data provision goes beyond mere numbers; it also includes policies and regulations. Present specific, measurable, and observable information, including survey data and results, without bias or preconceived notions. Ensure that all relevant data and comprehensive information are provided to strengthen understanding. Sharing partial information or one-sided perspectives can lead to greater confusion and misunderstandings. For instance, on social media platforms like WeChat, images lacking comprehensive context can easily lead to misinterpretations due to varying individual perspectives.

6. ***Paying Attention to Self and Others:*** Meaningful dialogue is facilitated when each group member is self-aware and conscious of others, understanding not only what they are

saying but also how they are saying it and how others are responding.

Cultivate self-awareness, self-understanding, self-management, and empathy. It is crucial to maintain a clear awareness of our own emotions and thoughts. Simultaneously, observe others' vocal patterns, expressions, and body language to stay attuned to their emotions. Maintain rationality and avoid becoming overly emotional in our responses. Additionally, to create an equal and open platform for everyone to speak, refrain from making subjective judgments. As the French writer Gustave Flaubert said: "There is no truth, there are only perceptions." Each of us perceives issues differently, and there is no absolute right or wrong. By shifting our perspective when considering a problem, we can realize that each person's viewpoint may be valid to varying degrees. For example, some parents may complain about inadequate school bus management or the quality of meals at the cafeteria. Viewing it from our own perspective, we might dismiss their concerns as nitpicking. However, considering it from the parents' standpoint, we can understand that they are expressing worries for their children's safety and well-being. By actively improving based on such understanding, both parties can ultimately benefit. The more we pay attention to ourselves and others, the more effective our communication and dialogue will be.

7. ***Presuming Positive Intentions:*** Assuming that others have positive intentions promotes and facilitates meaningful dialogue, eliminating unintentional put-downs.

Presuming positive intentions is the most fundamental prerequisite for any meaningful conversation. Believe that others have positive and constructive intentions, avoiding imposing negative motives on them. If we have already decided that someone is always sarcastic, troublesome, or looking for conflict, then the conversation with them is unlikely to yield positive results.

Consciously cultivate this as a regular practice rather than just a temporary effort or being passively receptive. Otherwise, we might feel uncomfortable and forced because we don't genuinely believe in the other person's positivity. Trust in the best aspects of others, acknowledging that even though they may have different views on a particular topic, they still share common goals and aim for a positive outcome.

This is the most powerful tool for managing any conflict, as it prevents disputes from escalating emotionally and allows discussions to stay at the cognitive level. By presuming positive intentions, you create a more harmonious and productive environment for effective communication and problem-solving.

Reflection

These are the seven strategies that I encountered back in 2007, and I have personally found them to be incredibly valuable over the years. That's why I'm excited to share them with you in this article. Now, I invite you to reflect on these questions:

- Which of these strategies do you already apply confidently in your daily interactions?
- Are there any specific strategies that you feel you need to consciously strengthen to become more effective in your communication?
- As you think about the examples we discussed earlier, do you notice any similar patterns in your own behavior?

How can you use these strategies to enhance your communication style and approach?

- Observe your colleagues and those around you. Do you see any of them exhibiting similar behavior? How do you think using these strategies could help improve the quality of dialogues or group discussions with them?

Role Play

The best way to learn effective communication strategies is through practice and role playing. Let's use Scenario #1 as an example to demonstrate how we would apply the strategies discussed in this article to deal with difficult issues. I encourage you to engage in role-playing with your colleagues, discuss the outcomes, and share your learnings with each other.

Scenario #1

An angry parent complains about the school bus not waiting for their child, who was only two minutes late, and demands the school cover the taxi fare.

In the role-play, one person will play the role of the angry parent, and another will take on the role of the school staff. As the parent, express your frustration about your child missing the school bus and demand the school to cover the taxi fare. The school staff should respond calmly and empathetically, inviting the parent to have a seat and acknowledging their feelings through paraphrasing.

The school staff should then give the parent enough time to explain the situation fully. Calmly explain the school's policies and the importance of following uniform times and management rules for all students. Use data and reasoning to emphasize the impact on other children's safety and timely arrival to class.

As the parent starts to understand the school's rationale, they should begin to calm down. The school staff should continue to presume positive intentions and avoid assuming any malicious intent. Focus on finding a resolution together through empathy and understanding.

Through effective communication and a calm demeanor, we should eventually lead to a resolution. The parent will appreciate being heard and understood, and as the parent, you will also realize the importance of following the school's policies for the collective well-being.

Remember, during the role play, try to fully embody the character and act out the scenario. After the role play, identify the strategies you used from the article and reflect on any additional strategies that may be helpful in each scenario. Below are the other scenarios:

Scenario #2

A parent refuses to wear an ID badge to enter the school, leading to a confrontation with the security guard, and then comes to you to resolve the issue.

Scenario #3

A new student's parent requests permission for their child to skip a grade.

Scenario #4

During a department meeting, one colleague keeps talking incessantly while others remain silent or show signs of impatience.

Now, it's your turn to practice and learn from these scenarios. Have fun role-playing and explore the power behind these seemingly simple communication strategies.

ESSAY #5

Drawing inspiration from the culture of a New Zealand rugby team and candidly sharing personal stories, Dan Brown aptly underscores the importance of non-teaching staff and highlights the value of diversity and inclusivity in building a thriving community. He emphasizes that every member of an organization, regardless of their role, plays a crucial part in its success.

Playing Your Part in Building an Inclusive Community

By Dan Brown

Director of Professional Learning and Development

Dulwich College, Singapore

Having lived in Singapore for over a decade, I have come to embrace life in Asia wholeheartedly. Here, I want to take a moment to commend our non-teaching staff for their invaluable contributions to our educational institutions. Often unappreciated, you are the unsung heroes who keep our schools running smoothly. When my head of college was out, and no one even knew, but when his assistant was away, everyone noticed.

Because my wife comes from New Zealand, I have spent a significant amount of time in that country recently, even though I am from the UK. In this article, I will draw inspiration from the celebrated culture of the New Zealand rugby team, the All Blacks, and emphasise the significance of embracing diversity to create a more inclusive environment.

The All Blacks stands as an exemplar of success in the sporting world. Extensive research has delved into the factors underpinning their remarkable achievements, and one vital aspect emerges: their culture. In the All Blacks, irrespective of their roles, everyone is regarded as an equal member of the team, including those working in non-player capacities such as the finance and marketing departments. After each victory, they exemplify their commitment to humility and teamwork by collectively cleaning the changing rooms and sweeping the floors. By cultivating a culture that rejects individual ego and superstar mentalities, the All Blacks has created an environment where every member accepts responsibility for any task, regardless of its size.

Another fascinating aspect of the All Blacks' culture stems from the Māori concept of "Whakapapa," which emphasises the importance of leaving a legacy for future generations. The team embraces several rituals, such as the pre-game ceremonial war dance known as the Hacker. Additionally, new players are presented with a black leather book containing pictures of the All Blacks' jerseys from different eras. Each page outlines the ethos, standards, morals, and expected behavior of those representing the team. The final page bears a profound statement: "Leave the Jersey in a better place." This principle encapsulates the idea that each person should strive to enhance the legacy of New Zealand rugby.

Recognising our collective responsibility enables us to surpass our individual roles. Whether in organisations, schools, or communities, our goal should always be to leave them in a better condition than we found them. A poignant example of the impact individuals can make lies in the actions of a group of hospital cleaners in the United States. These observant cleaners noticed that patients in a coma, recovering from cancer treatment, responded better to a stimulating environment. By rearranging and adding pictures, they created an engaging atmosphere. Subsequently, it was discovered that patients in their ward experienced faster recovery rates compared to other areas. This simple act of moving a picture demonstrates the transformative potential inherent in every individual to contribute to the betterment of our surroundings.

Allow me to share a personal experience that exemplifies the potential for positive change. Several years ago, I received an unexpected promotion offer at a school notorious for its poor reputation, having recently failed its inspection. Despite the daunting outlook, I chose to embrace the opportunity, driven by a desire to make a difference. The school's condition was disheartening, with crumbling buildings, unruly students, and underqualified teachers. Initially, I encountered significant challenges and contemplated giving up.

However, the unwavering support of a facilities manager named Dave sustained my resolve. Every evening, he would visit me, offering a cup of tea and some biscuits. We would chat, and he recognized that I was struggling and needed support. Dave's small acts of kindness and encouragement played a pivotal role, empowering me to persevere. Without Dave's support, I might have left the school and given up on my leadership role. Dave's encouragement gave me the strength to stay the course, and together with a dedicated team, we later achieved remarkable improvements, culminating in a successful inspection. This experience solidified my belief that every individual possesses the power to leave a place in a better condition than they found it.

Working in an international school has afforded me the privilege of engaging with diverse backgrounds, cultures, ethnicities, religions, and sexualities. Embracing this diversity is not without its challenges, as our ingrained beliefs and work styles may differ. However, it is precisely within this diversity that our greatest advantages lie. By taking the time to understand and appreciate other cultures, we can foster meaningful interactions and collaboration.

Let me share an example from my personal experience that highlights the importance of cultural understanding. Twelve years ago, I moved to Singapore for my wife's job, and I had to be a house husband for a few months. On the first day, my wife went to work, and I was left with our two children with nothing to eat. I heard about the hawker food centres (food courts) in Singapore and decided to take my kids there to experience Singaporean culture. Seeking directions, I approached the security guard at our condominium and asked him where the nearest hawker centre was. He kindly informed me that it was 1.5 kilometers away but advised me to take a taxi. Ignoring his advice, I embarked on the journey with my children, one in a buggy and the other on a scooter.

In no time, Singapore's relentless heat left me drenched in sweat. To make matters worse, a sudden and massive storm erupted, accompanied by lightning and thunder, which terrified my children. Amid the chaos, my son fell off his scooter and cut his knee, leaving me to deal with the blood and the crying children. By the time we arrived at the hawker food centre, we were soaking wet, but relieved to find an available table with a packet of tissue paper. Unaware of the local custom, I innocently sat down at the table and began using the tissue paper to clean up my children, assuming it was left there for communal use. To my surprise, a woman approached me angrily, claiming that I had stolen her table and her tissue paper. Perplexed, I tried to reason with her, questioning why she left the tissues on the table if they were meant solely for her use and how leaving them there indicated her ownership. I later learned that in Singapore, placing a packet of tissue paper on a table is a signal that you are "choping" or reserving the table for yourself. Regrettably, due to my exhaustion from an overnight flight and my lack of understanding of the cultural significance of the tissues, our conversation did not go well, resulting in unnecessary conflict.

By taking the time to learn about other cultures, we can gain a better understanding of our differences and find ways to work together more effectively. It's worth noting that even within a single culture, such as the UK, individuals may have vastly different experiences, making the dynamics even more complex. However, I believe that the key to navigate this complexity lies in building meaningful relationships.

If we aspire to have our voices heard and bring about positive changes that leave a lasting impact, developing strong relationships with others is absolutely essential. We must invest in getting to know people, understanding their backgrounds, and appreciating their unique perspectives. Recognising when they might be facing challenges or feeling stressed, just as Dave, the facilities manager at my school, did for me, can make the difference.

In conclusion, each one of us plays a crucial role in shaping a more inclusive and thriving community. Drawing inspiration from the All Blacks' culture of success, we can foster humility, teamwork, and a commitment to leaving a positive legacy. Additionally, by embracing diversity and taking the time to understand and appreciate different cultures, we can build stronger relationships and collaborate more effectively. Remember, our collective efforts, no matter how small, can have a profound impact on the journey toward a better, more inclusive future.

MY OTHER BOOKS ON AMAZON

Understanding China: An Insight into History, Civilization, and On-going Transformation

Book Author: Calipe Chong Wai Meng

Book Manager/Editorial Adviser: Henry Wong Yew Keong

The recent changes in China have been phenomenal. We have witnessed rapid development in industry and technology capabilities, alongside significant advancements in military power and foreign affairs. This book is authored by an overseas Chinese individual who has lived in China for more than 30 years. Originally from Singapore, he was initially employed by a major US tech company to work in China and now runs a successful business there.

The author does not intend to exaggerate China's achievements, nor is he glorifying its power and influence. Conversely, he does not aim to highlight its weakness or criticize its actions. Instead, he seeks to present an honest depiction of what China was like in the past, what it has experienced, and what it is now. The purpose of this book is to provide factual insights and real situations occurring in China that are often underreported in foreign countries.

Happily Married to a Chinese National: Practical Tips on Chinese-Foreign Relationships

Book Author: Multiple Authors

Book Manager/Editor: Henry Wong Yew Keong

This book is relevant for anyone in a cross-cultural or bi-national relationship, though it is also suitable for anyone in any kind of romantic relationship. It is written from a foreigner's perspective, with contributors hailing from the US, the UK, Singapore, New Zealand, Malaysia, and Canada. **Notably, forty percent of its contributors are international school educators.**

The authors address multiple issues found in marriages, particularly interracial and bi-national marriages, sharing their extensive experience in making cross-cultural relationships work. Topics include intercultural communication, conflict resolution, cultural differences, interacting with in-laws and relatives, raising children, living in a neutral third country, love and intimacy, and finances.

Effective Techniques for Part-Time Forex Traders

Book Author: Henry Wong Yew Keong

This book is specifically designed for novice part-time traders and aspiring professional traders. It is an excellent starting point for your forex trading journey. However, even if you already have some trading experience, you can still benefit from the additional techniques provided to increase your wins.

The author's intention is to make this book an easy read so that even newcomers to forex trading, without prior knowledge or experience, can follow along. It is not meant to be a comprehensive guide to FX trading; the purpose is to whet your appetite and get you started.

www.ingramcontent.com/pod-product-compliance
Lightning Source LLC
Chambersburg PA
CBHW071941210526
45479CB00002B/771